Breakdancing On A Balance Beam

How to Find Balance as a Business Person and
an Everything-Else-That-You-Are-Too Person

Kathy Frank

Illustrations by Caitlin Johnson-Nied

BaileyCourtCon Publishing, Bedminster, NJ

Breakdancing on a Balance Beam

Request for Information should be addressed to:
BaileyCourtCon Publishing, http://baileycourtcon.com
P.O. Box 7024, Bedminster, NJ 07921-7024
orders@baileycourtcon.com; +1-877-497-3369
Copyright © 2011 by Kathy Frank

All rights reserved. No part of this book may be reproduced or transmitted in any form or by any means, electronic or mechanical, including photocopying, recording, or by any information storage and retrieval system, without written permission from the author, except for the inclusion of brief quotations in a review.

International Standard Book Numbers
ISBN: 978-1-937788-02-5 – pbk – b/w
ISBN: 978-1-937788-00-1 – pbk – color
ISBN: 978-1-937788-07-0 – ebook

Library of Congress Cataloging-in-Publication Data

Frank, Kathy
Kathy Frank's breakdancing on a balance beam – how to be a businessperson and an everything-else-that you-are-too person
Includes bibliographical references and index.

2011917829

This book is dedicated to
my husband, **Peter**
who has always been the wind beneath my wings,
and is written in memory of my sister,
Geraldine O'Connor Mears
who lost her life too young.

What Others Are Saying...

"In today's hyper-competitive, hyper-fast or just plain "hyper" world, it's the rare individual who has the ability to help others look past the chaos and find ways to refocus on what's truly important. Kathy Frank is one of those people. I've worked with Kathy and members of her team for many years now. She has a unique personal style which simultaneously conveys both calmness and tenacity. Her ability to take the long view while working with you to deal with the immediately urgent is legendary. But most importantly, and as her book shows, she has a knack for making the growth in one's self awareness fun! This is a book for anyone who has ever wondered how they'll get through another personal crisis, work emergency, or family drama. But mostly, it's a tonic for anyone who wants some great ideas on how to look at life in a much more balanced way."

— **Steve Miranda,** Former Chief Human Resources Officer, Society for Human Resource Management (SHRM)

"Inspiring people leadership is a hallmark of all great organizations – indeed attracting, developing and retaining the very best people is often the difference between exceptional endeavors and the merely ordinary. *Breakdancing on a Balance Beam* – an experience-based offering from a truly distinctive people leader – is a veritable "how-to" guide for understanding and inspiring the modern workforce, mixing a unique brand of real-world applicability with powerful insights regarding human behavior. This book should be mandatory reading for anyone who has the opportunity and privilege to lead."

— **David C. Frank**, General Manager, Axiom Law, and former Partner at McKinsey & Company

"Balance is the word that I like to use most to describe how to be successful, whether as a business leader, parent or spouse. *Breakdancing on a Balance Beam* is a collection of both light hearted stories that will make you smile, and profoundly provocative messages. It is a prescription for the chaos that so often keeps us from remembering what's really important!

— **Dave Hickey,** President, Boon Corporation

"Kathy has been a mentor, a guide and a friend throughout tumultuous events in my business and personal life. *Breakdancing on a Balance Beam* comes directly from her heart. It is a personal anthology from one of the most gifted observers of human behavior of our times."

— **Sally Muscarella,** President, Interactive Media

What Others Are Saying...

"When I read and re-read Kathy Frank's nuggets of wisdom, my pulse slows and my breathing evens out. It's rare to find a book that you can dip into, always coming away enriched and invigorated – yet also relaxed and renewed. As a wife and mother, entrepreneur and writer, I often try to cram as much work as I can into short chunks of time. The stories, quotes, allegories and metaphors in *Breakdancing on a Balance Beam* remind me to slow down and take stock of what's most important to me."

— **Michelle Cameron**, Author of The Fruit of Her Hands, Associate Director of The Writers Circle

"I have seen firsthand how Kathy Frank can help individuals and groups understand themselves as a basis for working together happily and effectively. The same insight, creativity, sensitivity and humor that make her so good in helping others be their best selves comes through every page of *Breakdancing on a Balance Beam*. This is a book that makes you smile, if not laugh, at the same time you are introduced to fresh new ways of looking at life and the people who make it interesting and fun."

— **Charles L. Currie, S.J.** Former President of the Association of Jesuit Colleges and Universities

"Several months after we went public in 1996, Kathy introduced her organization to us. We were building and evolving our senior management team at that time and were struggling to move quickly, with purpose. Kathy enabled us to focus our energies, figure out what really mattered and helped us to build strong relationships among the team. It is wonderful to see her sage counsel in writing. This is a great resource for any manager seeking personal growth and is intent on developing their leadership style!"

— **Michael Keating**, Senior Vice President, Suburban Propane

"Fun, quick, with plenty of take home value is how I describe the new book, *Breakdancing On A Balance Beam*, by Kathy Frank. Kathy's writings inspire the reader to reflect on the big picture of life with short stories that are familiar to all of us, down to earth and potent. More powerful when read a second and third time her musings help put in perspective things we know and usually take for granted. The topics make for great dinner conversation with family and, as a parent, I know there are lessons being conveyed to the children without preaching."

— **David Strauss**, President, Key Container

What Others Are Saying...

"I engaged Kathy Frank several years ago as a consultant to assist our organization. She has been both an effective consultant and a friend. One of the many benefits I receive from working with Kathy is her monthly newsletter. Reading Kathy's newsletters over the years, has shown me that she understands many of my everyday challenges, in both my personal and my work life. It is amazing how often I have found myself struggling in an area and soon after I see that Kathy's next newsletter has arrived in my e-mail box and it is addressing the very challenge that I am dealing with. I strongly recommend Kathy and her book to anyone who is looking for a little inspiration and some insight into how to better manage their own life's challenges."

— **Maureen Finn**, *Divisional Director of Human Resources, Ametek*

"I love books that both entertain and enlighten with insightful stories that come from real life...which is why I love *Breakdancing on a Balance Beam* -- a compilation of punchy, fun loving stories that will ring true to your heart."

— **W. Bradford Swift,** *Author of Life On Purpose:*
Six Passages to an Inspired Life
Co-Founder, Life On Purpose Institute

"Our hectic schedules make it difficult to find time to consciously think about our strengths and weaknesses, and how our behaviors impact others; especially when we are tired, angry or frustrated. Sometimes, just hearing someone else's story will give us a new perspective or remind us of one we've forgotten. Kathy Frank is a gifted storyteller who seems to find inspiration in everyone and everything and I'm thankful that she has taken the time to share her insights."

— **Leslie Segal, CEO,** *Testware Associates, Inc.*

"I've grown to rely on Kathy to help me better understand, avoid and overcome many challenges I've run into in my businesses over the past decade. Kathy's unique experience and perspective come to life in "Breakdancing on a Balance Beam;" it's a 'must-have' for entrepreneurs and business owners seeking to navigate through their journey at work and at home with confidence!"

— **Graeme Bradley, CEO,** *The Eleven Agency (T11A)*

What Others Are Saying...

"For two decades, my colleagues and I have benefited from Kathy Frank's insightful techniques to develop people, relationships and organizations. Her creative and innovative approaches to understanding the complexities of how people engage with one another have helped me value their individual strengths and have led me to more informed business decisions and deeper personal friendships. Kathy offers balanced perspectives on business, life and family that have helped make me a more skillful business partner and a better person."

— **Alfred K. Potter II,** *Senior Vice President, Gilbane Building Company*

"This book is a must-read for those people looking for solid, practical advice on how to effectively manage the ever-elusive work-life balancing act! The humor and advice make you laugh and think at the same time while allowing the reader to absorb information in large or small portions! It's brilliant!"

— **Allison M. Wollen**, *Corporate Vice President, Human Resources, University of Massachusetts Health Alliance Hospital*

"Kathy Frank has hit a home run with her new book! Weaving together what she has learned as an entrepreneur, wife, mother and passionate lover of life, she's created a fun, readable book full of thought-provoking and inspirational ideas about work and life."

— **Andrea Novakowski**, *Business Coach*

"Anyone who has worked with Kathy will know that with her great wisdom comes a speed of talking that is unmatched. It is nice to see her words in print where I can keep up with them! I continue to be amazed with Kathy's insights and generosity. She has a terrific way of delivering feedback to clients that is on target and actionable. She doesn't just offer the "what" but the "what to do about it." This book is just a small example of her wisdom and wit. I highly recommend engaging with Kathy, even if only in writing...."

— **Kim Carpenter**, *Vice President, Human Resources, Covidien Surgical Devices*

"This book is everything that has been learned, realized and accomplished by one of the most insightful and inspirational people I've ever known. Amazing person...amazing book"

— ***Tracey Rietema**, Director-Operations, Rienzi & Rienzi Communications*

FOREWORD	**12**
PREFACE	**15**
USING THIS BOOK	**17**
FINDING (AND KEEPING) YOUR INNER CHILD	**21**
I Deleted Them For Awhile But Now They Are Back	23
The Rhythm Is the Beat	25
The Sounds of the Season	27
Sand Castles	29
TAKING A TIME OUT	**33**
A Silo in the Field	35
Lost and Found	37
Let It Be	39
Weight Limit	41
Tempus Fugit (Time Flies)	43
PLAYING NICELY WITH OTHERS	**47**
Competition or Collaboration?	49
Listen and Learn	53
What Is a Silo Anyway?	55
Winners Hit the Ground Running!	57
STEPPING UP TO THE PLATE	**61**
It's All About Trust	63
Accountability	66
The Essence of Style	69
Redefining that Competitive Edge	71

Tee It Up!	74
Coaching For All Ages	76
Contemplating Courage	78

HANGING IN THERE	**83**
In the Black	85
Count Me In	87
Take a Look Inside	89
"Got No Checkbooks, Got No Banks"	91
A Painted Sky	93

BEING OPEN TO CHANGE	**97**
Embracing Change	99
Opportunities Versus Obstacles	101
The Art of Selling Change	103
Out-of-the-Box Thinkers	105

COMMUNICATING EFFECTIVELY	**109**
The Medium Is the Message. Or Is It?	111
Music Speaks Volumes	114
A, B, Triple C	116
Are They Really As They Seem?	119

BEING ABLE TO LAUGH	**123**
Laughing Can Be the Best Treat!	125
The Value of a Smile	127
Laughter is the Shortest Distance	129
Metrics: Do They Always Measure Up?	132

BEING OPEN TO POSSIBILITIES	**137**
As High As A Kite	139
Slightly Out Of Sync	142
Maximize YOUR Impact	144
A Clear Forecast	146
The Bridge Is Out!	147
On a Wing and a Prayer	149
A Light at the End of the Tunnel	151
VALUING CREATIVITY AND INNOVATION	**155**
Creativity: The New C and the Box	157
YART Sale	160
Great Teachers and Great Artists	162
What Is a Lemon?	165
BELIEVING IN YOURSELF	**169**
An Invisible, But Powerful, Force	171
Hire Power	173
A View From the Top	176
An Inspiration	178
The Entrepreneur in All of Us	180
Playing the Game	183
EPILOGUE	**188**
ABOUT THE AUTHOR	**190**
ACKNOWLEDGEMENTS	**191**

Foreword

When I first met Kathy Frank, I was a skeptic. She had come to administer a behavioral assessment survey to the members of the management staff at the company where I work. We'd undergone a considerable trauma, the unexpected death of our founder and president. His wife, who had bravely stepped in to take the reins, wanted to address the lingering stress our team was feeling.

I was skeptical that any survey could accurately gauge my personality, especially in relationship to the team. I was not interested in spending the day forced to do team building exercises. I just wanted to be left alone with the enormous pile of work I had to contend with.

But one session with Kathy Frank was enough to make a believer out of this skeptic. Her cheerful, matter-of-fact manner and the way she was able to read us all was astonishing. And her ability to make a significantly demoralized team feel that we actually could manage to work together was, quite honestly, nothing short of a miracle.

It speaks volumes to Kathy's own personality that, when I continued to struggle with my personal choices at work, she was one of the first people I called. As Kathy herself would tell you, it wasn't a risk I would normally take – but something about Kathy Frank made it feel safe. Her advice was sound, and she helped me make some risky but ultimately rewarding choices. Like so many other people, I am blessed to call Kathy a friend as well as a trusted business advisor.

Yet, when she asked me to write the Foreword for *Breakdancing on a Balance Beam,* I was taken aback. Flattered, sure. But uncertain. You don't generally find me browsing the inspirational bookshelves in the book store. Here, too, the skeptic in me emerged.

But as I began to read the short musings that Kathy selected to be included in this volume, I realized that she was talking directly to me. To me as a working wife and mother, as a woman with creative aspirations, as someone who has a yen to live life on her own terms. And especially now, to me as I embrace a new episode in my own life as an entrepreneur.

Some of my favorites? There are so many. I loved Kathy's essay on "Tempus Fugit" (Time Flies) because it's so easy to become overwhelmed, to forget the simple joys in life – and Kathy reminded me of some of the most basic. Her "Out-of-the-Box Thinkers" made me reconsider what type of environment can balance both structure and creativity. Because I'm trying to be both a great teacher *and* a great artist, naturally "Great Teachers and Great Artists" spoke to me loud and clear. And as someone who sat back for too long and yearned for change, "Hire Power" made me recall that I'm the person in charge of my own life, no one else.

Every time I pick up *Breakdancing on a Balance Beam*, I find something new that I want to stop and contemplate. Kathy has a knack for finding the right quotations to motivate and inspire you. Her down-to-earth stories are valuable because of the mingled strands of common sense and aspiration that give you a starting point for your personal and professional ambitions – as well as a place to return to when you need to refresh and renew your goals.

But don't take my word for it, especially if you, like me, are a skeptic. Read on and find out for yourself.

Michelle Cameron
Author of *The Fruit of Her Hands* and *In the Shadow of the Globe*
Associate Director of The Writers Circle

Preface

"Your time is limited, so don't waste it living someone else's life....Don't let the noise of others' opinions drown out your own inner voice. And most important, have the courage to follow your heart and intuition. They somehow already know what you truly want to become. Everything else is secondary."

- Steve Jobs

When I was a child, I often organized my brothers and sisters to perform plays for our relatives. We'd sing and dance, and tumble like acrobats. I dreamed of someday becoming a great singer — but my vocal chords did not share that dream! And while I was a good athlete, I was no Mary Lou Retton. I have always been captivated by gymnasts — those nimble, strong athletes dancing their way across a balance beam. Perhaps because I grew up in the television age when we could see world class gymnasts performing live, my dreams have always taken me to a place of movement, grace and balance.

Growing up, I was enthralled by graceful dances and gymnastic routines. I envied those athletes who combined physical and emotional strength, poise, flexibility and mental discipline. In more recent times, those skills are combined in breakdancing — that high-energy contortionism that looks like a combination of dancing and what your body does when you hit a patch of ice on a ski slope.

Looking back, it's clear that I was not destined to become either a dancer or a gymnast. Instead, my life's journey took me on a different path. After a tour through several careers that just weren't good matches with who I am, I took to the road of entrepreneurship "...and that has made all the difference" (to quote Robert Frost). I discovered my true passion: running *my own* business.

Now that I'm older, more experienced and, I hope, a bit wiser, I think that my childhood dreams were preparation for all the ups and downs that life as a business owner throws at you. I have learned a lot and wanted to share what I learned. So I started writing a monthly newsletter — both as a way to share my experiences so others could learn from them without going through them and (practically speaking) as a way to keep in touch with my clients. What I didn't expect was that writing would become something I looked forward to each month. Plus, my clients started telling me how much they enjoyed reading them. I hope these newsletters will become a legacy — for my grandchildren and those I might have touched in some way over the years.

Kathy Frank

Using This Book

Albert Einstein said, "Life is like riding a bicycle. To keep your balance, you must keep moving." And Ann Morrow Lindbergh said: "A note of music gains significance from the *silence* on either side."

Breakdancing on a Balance Beam is all about the music of life and the peace of silence — and finding the equilibrium between the two.

The thoughts collected in this book are grouped according to the skills and knowledge I've found essential for achieving balance in my life. You don't have to read it straight through — you can visit it from time to time for perspective, when you need a lift or need to see how someone else has dealt with a similar problem or challenge. You may want to start with a topic in the middle or others at the end. It really doesn't matter. Balance is about capitalizing on our ups and downs and learning how each of them can teach us life's lessons. The key is to find what works for you.

This book is divided into 11 Chapters, which contain what I call Musings. Webster's definition of *musing (verb)* is to become absorbed in thought, or to turn something over in your mind. The ancient Greeks saw a *muse* (noun) as someone who could reveal knowledge through storytelling. So I have created my Musings as specific stories or occurrences which lead to thoughts and insights that I hope you find helpful in achieving your own balance.

Here are the Musings that I've been turning over in my mind throughout my career building a business.

Finding and Keeping your Inner Child.

The child within is always talking to us. How often do we listen? As we get older why is it so hard to *Find and Keep Our Inner Child?*

Taking a Time Out.

The silence between the notes is essential for everyone's well being for getting in the proper rhythm of life. How often do we take the time to really enjoy the silence of *Taking A Time Out*?

Playing Nicely With Others.

What happens when you have no choice — you have to play with someone you just can't stand? Is it possible they march to a different drummer than you do and that you are meant to learn something from them that will help you grow as a person and *Play Nicely With Others?*

Stepping Up to the Plate.

We must all be accountable for our actions, at home and at work, but it's not always easy or comfortable. Why is *Stepping Up To The Plate* often scary and difficult to do?

Hanging In There.

We all have our days, weeks or months when life throws us curve balls we didn't expect. In this moment in time, how can we dig deep to find the courage and strength to just *Hang In There*?

Being Open to Change.

"Every day is a fresh beginning; and each morn is the world made new." Change is always with us. So why is it that *Change* is something we often resist? What might happen if we put more effort into *Being Open To Change* than resisting it?

Communicating Effectively.

Communication is a two-way street. What happens when you're on the same street but going in opposite directions? Why is it that *Communicating Effectively* can often hit so many road blocks?

Being Able To Laugh.

Laughter is often the best medicine — and the health benefits of a good laugh cannot be overstated. So why is it that we don't make time each day to *Find That Laughter*?

Being Open to Possibilities.

Why do we often seem to settle for the routine and ordinary, when there are so many EXTRAORDINARY possibilities out there?   What might happen if we *Open Our Minds To Those Unlimited Possibilities*?

Valuing Creativity and Innovation.

Creativity lies within each one of us.   How can we value *Creativity and Innovation* if we're afraid to try it ourselves?

Believing In Yourself.

My final reflection in this book is very near and dear to my heart: *Believing in Yourself.* Sometimes attaining and sustaining belief in ourselves feels like trying to breakdance on a balance beam — a constant need to change direction, modify goals and behaviors and adapt to the unplanned while maintaining the attitude *of Believing In Yourself.* How can we all learn to accept and celebrate our uniqueness?

At the end of each Musing , I've included a place where you can jot down YOUR THOUGHTS on a Balance Beam and stop for a few minutes, reflect on what you have just read and look inside yourself.

We are all Breakdancing everyday on a Balance Beam to our own beat and to our own rhythm. Taking the time to sort through your thoughts and write them down very often is the key to finding the balance and staying on the beam.

FINDING (AND KEEPING) YOUR INNER CHILD

When we are children life is spontaneous, non-stop, and lived in the moment. Our brains are not yet cluttered with the details of living — and I believe our thoughts are clear and purposeful. As we grow up, for whatever reason, we sometimes lose that clarity and purpose. Why? How can we regain the childhood vision that time has clouded?

Here are some thoughts about the value of re-connecting with the elements of childhood: the ability to cope when things don't go our way, the joy of friendship, keeping a sense of wonder, remembering to have fun.

I Deleted Them For Awhile But Now They Are Back

When my grandson, Connor, was six years old, his Mom asked why he hadn't been playing with his friends Sean and Kara. Connor replied, "I deleted them for a while, but now they're back." Welcome to the 21st Century: The Millennium Generation, and the era of computers, texting, and new ways of communicating! Question: Would children of the Silent Generation, Baby Boomers, Gen X or Gen Y have spoken with their parents or schoolmates in such engagingly provocative jargon? The styles and norms of communication differ widely from generation to generation, based on the developments and technology of that era. We are products of our time and environment.

It is important to embrace the wisdom and values of the generations that precede and follow our own. Do not push aside those who came before us — they possess a wealth of knowledge and experience that can make life more rich, connected, and meaningful. Children are our ears and eyes to the future, but we may not always listen to their message. We may dismiss the voice of young people with thoughts such as, "What do they know — they're just kids!"

FINDING AND KEEPING YOUR INNER CHILD

One thing remains constant throughout the generations: Change happens whether we want it to or not. Although the jargon of communication is a product of its time, each generation benefits when they learn to appreciate and understand the values and perspectives of others. These learnings help us navigate our own life's journey.

In our modern world, the diversity of communication styles, the size of the world's population, and the amount of information that bombards us each day has grown (and will continue to grow) exponentially. Members of The Silent Generation tend to prefer tangible items, e.g., the feel of a book or newspaper. Baby Boomers value competition, and blend tradition with technology. Gen X and Gen Y place a high value on technology and rely on its tools for communicating and multi-tasking. The new Millennial Generation is strictly high tech and moving at a pace faster than anyone could have imagined in the 1930s, 60s, or 90s!

The words of Elton John — "There's far too much to take in here" — in the song "Circle of Life" from *The Lion King,* reminds us that we need each other and can learn from one another. Each of us has gifts to offer. Imagine how we could benefit from relying on one another, listening and accepting our differences.

Mahatma Gandhi said, "We must be the change we want to see in the world whether we are 6 or 96. If we listen with understanding to the differences — as well as the similarities — of those who came before and after us, we will learn to bridge the gap between the generations and achieve a synergy that will benefit us all." Thank you, Connor, for being you!

The Rhythm Is The Beat

"I couldn't enjoy my work if I walked to someone else's rhythm."
- Daniel Day Lewis

Every minute in hospitals throughout the world, a miracle of life happens: A baby is born! Infants coo, smile, and cry out to be fed. As these babies mature into childhood, they are naturally adventurous, seizing life and all it has to offer.

Along the way, however, rules and structure are imposed on a child's search for understanding and knowledge. Some parameters are necessary to protect children from harm; but sometimes restrictions are imposed by well-meaning adults who want the child to do things their way. Any parent knows that, in the long run, you cannot control a child's life search. Children will always gravitate towards what is natural for them — it's in their core; it is part of who they are. When kids are encouraged to explore their true identity early in life, they will learn their own rhythm rather than listening to a rhythm that belongs to someone else.

Daniel Day-Lewis is a celebrated actor, sought after by major film directors. He is selective about the roles he accepts because he strives to keep a balance in his life by allocating time to what is important to him. He understands his own rhythm and then chooses activities that allow him to beat to it — to do what is best for him.

FINDING AND KEEPING YOUR INNER CHILD

As adults and leaders, we must find ways to nurture that child within us to resurrect the creativity, inquisitiveness, and sense of wonder we once had. Games such as golf, tennis, football, and soccer require practice, timing, creativity, discipline, and precision. So too does life — but it is *our life*. Like Daniel Day-Lewis, we need to fully understand our goals and dreams, and listen to the rhythm of our own lives. The key to success in any venture is to be who we are and gravitate to the things we love and enjoy. At the same time we must always respect differences in others. The integration of the self with others makes life magical and gives a special rhythm that is unique to each of us!

The Sounds Of The Season

At Halloween, we like to conjure up age old images that scared us as children. And yet, when we answer the door on Halloween night to greet the costumed children, our spirits lighten and we pick up on their sense of fun. They are excited about dressing up in costume — Darth Vader, the Wicked Witch of the East (or West), a pirate, or Little Red Riding Hood, a ghost, or goblin, to name a few! They are exploring new adventures and experiencing new thrills.

Many adults wish they could recapture the innocence of their youth — to be open to new ideas and experiences and to be more spontaneous. As we mature, openness and spontaneity often slip away, replaced by grownup responsibilities and attitudes. Of course, to survive and succeed in the modern adult world, we cannot revert to childish ways; but we *can* strive for a childlike openness to new ideas, adventures and fun. Here are some questions to read our "childlike" barometer:

- Have I checked in with myself lately?
- Who and where am I?
- Am I having fun searching for new experiences?
- Am I enjoying myself and what I have become?

FINDING AND KEEPING YOUR INNER CHILD

I recently attended a workshop where Alan Weiss, author of the book *Million Dollar Consulting*, was the speaker. He had the audience in the palm of his hand with his knowledge, business acumen and outstanding sense of humor. It was clear from the outset that Alan's passion and sense of fun are the reasons he excels at what he does. He projected sincerity and a fullness of life. What a gift — to engage a roomful of 250 people; every one enjoying themselves, learning, and laughing loud and hard. Alan not only made *others* laugh — he had the childlike quality of laughing at *himself*.

> "The person who knows how to laugh at
> himself will never cease to be amused."
> - Shirley MacLaine

Just as we did at Halloween as children, so today we can take any opportunity to laugh, seek out new adventures, and have some fun. Openness, spontaneity, optimism and passion are the tricks and treats of being in a childlike state of mind in a very adult world.

Sand Castles

If you've ever watched children building a sand castle on the beach, you've seen them running, laughing, jumping, tussling, whispering secrets and even yelling at each other. Some kids are great communicators in an open setting — others prefer to work by themselves; some give directions — others like to sit back and watch; some like to dive right in. Others want to consider if it's okay to take the plunge. When the tide rises, some will stand up and scream — others will just sit back and watch. Each child is unique even in a common activity — they are being themselves by acting naturally.

Eventually kids grow up and the sand castles become careers. However, the principles of working together and accepting each other's differences remain the same at all stages of life. It is important to understand and value those differences — whether building a sand castle, a career or a business. In adult life, we need the right people in the right roles at the right time for an activity to function well — be it an organization, a war-time effort or a philanthropic endeavor. We also need to understand and value the diversity required for such success. What is right for one sand castle builder may not be right for another, but when both builders work together — respecting their differences and combining their strengths — the result can be a unique and impressive structure that makes a difference in the world.

FINDING AND KEEPING YOUR INNER CHILD

When organizations are small, people need to be adaptable — to bend and flow; digging the moat at the same time they raise the ramparts. As an organization grows, structure and process replace the old way of doing things. If people within the organization have not raised the bar for their own skill sets, the organization will fill the gap by hiring people who have the needed skills. As we mature and age, the structure, rules and norms we adopted along the way can block us from reaching our full potential. Just as conditions on a beach determine the right type of sand castle, conditions in a business will determine the right person for each role. To be successful, we must adapt to the changing environment while honoring those innate characteristics that make each of us unique. The challenge for the general contractors of "sand castles" is to respect and value differences, while blending them to create a structure that all can appreciate: The whole is greater than the sum of its parts.

We are entering a new paradigm in the world order with new rules and dynamics. No matter where your organization is right now, think back to that (now grownup) child in you and make the decision that is — and always has been — the right one for *you*. Celebrate your uniqueness, but be open to change. Be aware of how the tide is turning, and adjust yourself for success. In the end, that *Inner Child* really does know the right thing for you to do to grow, change, flourish and enjoy yourself — whatever the circumstances!

Finding And Keeping Your Inner Child

The child within is always talking to us. How often do we listen? As we get older why is it so hard to Find and Keep Our Inner Child?

FINDING AND KEEPING YOUR INNER CHILD

TAKING A TIME OUT

Whoa! Hold on there Speedy Ladder Climber! In your race to The Top, have you forgotten about the importance of taking a timeout? Have you lost sight of the need to re-charge your personal batteries regularly?
I did...for awhile.

Then I began to think about what exactly I was proving by working 60- to 90-hour weeks. I certainly wasn't becoming happier or more successful, really. What I was becoming was burned out. So I started writing down my thoughts about why it is important to take a timeout — a vacation, a journey away from your goals for a short while, be it 5 minutes or 5 months.

BREAKDANCING ON A BALANCE BEAM

A Silo In The Field

Once while driving in the countryside on a quiet and idyllic Sunday morning, out of the corner of my eye I noticed a silo sitting in a beautiful field. I wished I had the time to stop and enjoy the simple serenity of the scene. However, time was pressing and so I continued on my way and made a turn back onto busy Main Street, USA.

Life is a journey with many twists, turns, and stops — all of which may lead us to places we've never been before...if we are open to the possibilities. When we fail to take the time to drink in those "scenes in the countryside," we may be depriving ourselves of beautiful insights and elegant solutions for some vexing problems. As Michelangelo observed: "I saw the angel in the marble, and carved until I set it free." Before he began carving, he had to take the time to think and observe the possibilities in the marble.

Be open and alive to the possibilities that surround you. Explore and discover new places with family and friends. Plan to do activities that recharge your batteries and spirits! Enjoy them to the fullest — especially the simplest and most obvious of the beauties and insights...the ones we take for granted or overlook entirely in our day-to-day lives.

TAKING A TIME OUT

Today a popular concept in business is "breaking down silo mentalities" to improve communication across organizations. In general, I support that approach and the work that helps to achieve it. However, not all silos are bad! There are moments in our hectic day when we can benefit from a visit to that silo in the beautiful field to enjoy its serenity, peace and calm.

Enjoy the silos! Leave your computer, iPad® and *BlackBerry*® behind (or, if you must, restrict them to very limited, defined periods of use) and reconnect with the essentials of life — human relationships and the beauty of nature in all its guises.

Lost And Found

"You may delay but time will not."
- Benjamin Franklin

"You don't drown by falling in the water. You drown by staying there."
- Author Unknown

Work in the technology age has become overloaded with information and stress. *So much to do; so little time.* The irony is: When we lose control of time by worrying or complaining that we just can't keep up with it or even find it, then we totally miss out on what's really important. Notice how often we equate life with time. Ben Franklin said, "If you love life, then do not squander time for that is the stuff life is made from." *Time waits for no one.* Each second that we fail to make our own is lost forever.

We all have moments when we feel overwhelmed and lost. We may feel that we're continually treading water, fighting time and just trying to hang on. Yet, if we listen, try to relax and let go, we might find that inner strength to surface and catch our breath!

TAKING A TIME OUT

When I teach, I often ask the question: *How many of you like to go on vacation?* Needless to say, all hands are raised. Then I ask: *What is it about a vacation that makes you want to take it?* Most often the answer is: "Because then we can find time to just do what we want to do." But wait — why can't that decision be ours every day? Aren't life's choices individual and ongoing? Why do we have to wait a whole year before we can find time to relax and enjoy what we want to do? Stop! Let us remember that time is an artificial device for measuring how our lives are lived. It is a measure; but not the only, most important measure. It is useful for knowing when to sow and when to reap; when to dress warm and bring in the firewood. We cannot focus so much on time that we overlook what is truly important — how we live our lives.

If we constantly think about lost time, we will never find the present-day possibilities and adventures — the gifts that can turn things around and make all the difference. Instead of spending time looking *back* (or, for that matter, looking *forward*), take the present gift of time. Use it well and make things happen for you and those around you — your family, friends, colleagues, and employees.

Let It Be

Recently I was working on a last-minute project and needed a reference from a specific book to complete the project. I placed a call to the local bookstore and was told they had one copy in stock. I jumped into my car and rushed over to pick it up.

When I arrived at the bookstore moments later, the clerk told me the book was not available. Needless to say, I became impatient and frustrated. I asked the clerk whether the book could have been misplaced or sold in the short 15 minutes since I had called the store. He answered that the computer still indicated that the store had one copy in stock. Together we looked for that book up and down the store aisles, but our efforts proved fruitless. It was one of those moments when you just want to scream! However, I kept my anger in check…but felt even more frustrated —@#$@%!!!

At that moment, I heard The Beatles' song "Let It Be" playing in the background. The lyrics and soft melody had an immediate calming effect on me, and I began to relax. I remember thinking, "Maybe that book just wasn't meant to be. It's only a book —albeit a special one — but, in reality, I can make do with an alternative book."

TAKING A TIME OUT

As I approached the checkout counter with my alternative book, I happened to bump into the woman who had recommended the original book to me. We started talking and I explained my plight. She smiled at me and said, "I am the culprit who took your book. I have it here in my cart. Whenever I am in a bookstore and I see a copy of it, I always buy it to share with a friend. Today, my friend, it is clearly meant to be *yours*." She then handed me the book and said, "Take it and enjoy it with my compliments."

The moral of this story is: Life is full of alternatives. Alternative thinking helps us cope with frustrating situations. Sometimes we become so focused on one issue that we lose sight of the big picture. If we stop, look and listen, we will find acceptable alternatives and people who can help us. When you find yourself in those situations, just relax and *let it be*.

Weight Limit

While driving on a country road last week, I glanced to my right and saw a sign that read, "Weight Limit 4 Tons". It slowed me down. I interpreted that message as a reminder that I had better go on a diet and lose those extra pounds — before I close in on that 4-ton mark! (Those inspiring emails from Weight Watchers® never looked so good!)

Most of us are working 24/7 trying to balance the commitments of work and family...and time (oh, that most elusive element). This demanding balancing act makes us feel like we are carrying an enormous weight — even if our weight is within the acceptable range on the height and weight charts or the BMI (Body Mass Index) calculator. The stresses of modern life catch up to all of us in one way or another at some point in our lives and take different forms; for example, overeating (or eating poorly), lack of exercise, fractured personal relationships. If we are lucky, at some point we realize the problem and say, "It's time to step back and appreciate what I have!"

From time to time, it's important to take stock of what we have achieved, and consider ways we can lighten our load in the future. *When we step back, we free ourselves*

TAKING A TIME OUT

to move forward. The turn of each season is a perfect time to renew our strength, confidence, and commitment by reflecting on where we have been, where we are now, and where we want to go — and how to get there with zest and enthusiasm.

Living in a goal-oriented society, we sometimes forget to pause and listen to the insights of wise people, such as Gandhi: "...salvation lies in the effort, not in the attainment. Full effort is full salvation."

A "4-ton weight" takes on different shapes for different people. Each of us needs to begin letting go of *our* "4-ton weight" before we exceed our own limits. Begin by taking deep breaths and creating time and space for yourself to think, relax and play.

Tempus Fugit (Time Flies)

When time is the perceived enemy — and the seconds, minutes, and hours tick away — we can often let the pressures build and overwhelm us, thereby spending even more time *worrying* and less time *doing*.

We live in a world of constant change and chaos. As the global economy lurches and the world order changes, the smiles on peoples' faces dissipate, replaced by expressions of apprehension and worry. Many people are nervous about the future and let fear — that most useless of emotions — overtake and rob them of the one precious thing that never stops rushing on: *Time*.

> "Make sure our attitude determines our life; never let our life determine our attitude"
> -Anonymous

When things are tough — trying to make ends meet, providing for ourselves and our families, paying the bills — our attitude and actions can make all the difference. A positive attitude can turn time into a catalyst for hope and

TAKING A TIME OUT

new beginnings, rather than the inexorable ticking away of our dreams and our future. As the political candidates chant "change is the answer" for our country, we can reflect on the changes *we* need to make in our daily lives that can make them better, richer and more worthwhile.

The smiles on children's faces; the pets that love us — regardless of the kind of day we've had; the flowers blooming in the spring; the laughter and camaraderie of friends; a stream flowing freely; the mountains so high and valleys so low; the thank you from a colleague; the gracious hand that reaches out to help when we least expect it...all of these things bring a sense of hope, peace, quiet and renewal into our world in the midst of seemingly constant turmoil. When time appears to be the enemy, think about changing your attitude and taking action.

Time is a metaphor for life, but it is not life. Time is spent by action or, sadly, inaction. We must act wisely! Remember, the little things in life make all the difference. Why not create those moments in time so they can be treasures for a lifetime?

> "Time is free, but it is priceless. You can't own it, but you can use it. You can't keep it, but you can spend it. Once you've lost it, you can never get it back."
> — Harvey Mackay

BREAKDANCING ON A BALANCE BEAM

Taking A Time Out

The silence between the notes is essential for everyone's well being for getting in the proper rhythm of life. How often do we take the time to really enjoy the silence of Taking A Time Out?

TAKING A TIME OUT

PLAYING NICELY WITH OTHERS

"No man is an island entire of itself;
every man is a piece of the continent,
a part of the main..."
- John Donne 1572-1631

For many of us, our ability to get along with others is a critical — and often challenging — skill. Also, it is likely that, at some point in our careers, we will need to work with someone that we, frankly, just can't stand. What do we do? How can we get along? Why can't we get along?? How can we turn the conflict of mismatched egos into a team?

Over the years, I have given considerable thought to the dynamics of teams and teamwork. My hope is that the following reflections will spark some ideas of your own — which you can then share with your teammates, co-workers, and other pieces of your "continent, a part of the main...."

BREAKDANCING ON A BALANCE BEAM

Competition Or Collaboration?

Winning at all costs
Competing alone
The individual is where it all begins

versus

Winning as a team
Competing together
Together we can accomplish more

ALL GOING FOR THE GOLD!

Which is more beneficial for organizations?

Competition and collaboration are not mutually exclusive. First, an organization must decide the goals it wants to achieve. Then it can establish the rules and incentives it believes necessary to achieve those results. With collaboration, the incentive for the participants is primarily the overall end result of the project;

for example, Rodgers & Hammerstein. With competition, the incentive for the players is primarily personal satisfaction and fulfillment, for example, Tiger Woods. Isn't the world a richer and more interesting place with both?

A successful partnership between collaboration and competition helps companies get creative ideas off the ground. Great ideas matter only if they are implemented. Groups with a high degree of competition tend to perform better on complex, high-creativity tasks because new ideas come quicker and faster. However, if the competition becomes negative, then it can lead to team breakdown or team members lacking confidence to share ideas. On the other hand, collaborative teams are good at getting straightforward tasks done efficiently and effectively. However, there is danger in the development of "groupthink", where ideas are not challenged and everyone just goes with the flow.

Below are some thoughts from people of varied backgrounds on this topic:

> "If you're not making mistakes, you're not taking risks, and that means you're not going anywhere. The key is to make mistakes faster than the competition, so you have more chances to learn and win."
> - John W. Holt, Jr.

> "The essence of competitiveness is liberated when we make people believe that what they think and do is important - and then get out of their way while they do it."
> - Jack Welch

> "Competition creates better products; alliances create better companies."
> - Brian Graham

> "Great discoveries and improvements invariably involve the cooperation of many minds. I may be given credit for having blazed the trail, but when I look at the subsequent developments I feel the credit is due to others rather than to myself."
> - Alexander Graham Bell

> "If you want to be incrementally better: Be competitive. If you want to be exponentially better: Be cooperative."
> — Unknown

> "The lightning spark of thought generated in the solitary mind awakens its likeness in another mind."
> — Thomas Carlyle

> "Many ideas grow better when transplanted into another mind than the one where they sprang up."
> — Oliver Wendell Holmes

> "If you have an apple and I have an apple and we exchange these apples, then you and I will still each have one apple. But if you have an idea and I have an idea and we exchange these ideas, then each of us will have two ideas."
> — George Bernard Shaw

What is the resolution?
Do we compete or do we collaborate?

On a daily basis, each of us must decide that answer both in the workplace and in our personal lives. Competition tends to be short-lived while collaboration can go on forever. We need the inspiration, insight, creativity and drive of the competitor; but many ideas, once conceived, can be implemented better by a collaborative group.

In the 21st Century world, given the interconnectedness of all people and the flood of available information, it is likely that competition (other than in individual sports such as golf, tennis, or seeking the next job promotion) will be between organized collaborative teams. The complexity and speed of the modern world will demand that people collaborate to be successful. There will always be a place for the individual genius and a need for leaders who can motivate, manage and drive the collaborative team; but the future is likely to be team, companies and countries

PLAYING NICELY WITH OTHERS

competing. Of course, such teams must be led by people with a vision who know how to achieve that vision and how to communicate that information to their teams in a collaborative way.

Listen And Learn

> "We learn more when we close our mouths and open our ears to really listen to the ideas and viewpoints of others."
> — Anonymous

Last week several of my colleagues and I sat down to work on a new initiative. My role was to provide the big picture view for the program, and their role was to bring the program to life by giving it the structure and depth of detail it sorely needed.

Several days later, my colleagues sent their first cut to me for feedback. Since the hours in that day had passed me by and I knew how important it was for them to receive my immediate feedback, I opted to give it a first pass at 1:00 AM — a time when I am never at my best and not thinking clearly.

As I read the first sentence, I went into "critic mode," which then blocked my ability to read the rest of the proposal with clarity and good judgment. In retrospect, I jumped into critic mode too quickly and was not able to give the proposal a fair assessment. The next day I told my colleagues I was not impressed with what I had read. They then asked me what part I took issue with, to which I replied, "All of it!"

PLAYING NICELY WITH OTHERS

After the look of shock on their faces subsided, we talked (and, at times, argued) it through. As I listened (really listened) to them (over a 3-hour time frame), it became clear that the initial sentence in each segment was the key stumbling block that needed to be changed. Once those changes were made, the remainder of the storyline made sense and was fun, creative, well planned, and well thought out.

Had my colleagues not been patient with me in taking the time to listen and explain their thinking and ideas, this program would have been trashed and we would have been back at the beginning.

Lessons learned:

> "*WE Are Smarter than ME*"
> - A book authored by Barry Libert and Jon Spector...and a very insightful thought!

> "Everyone needs to be heard and respected. They want it and you need it."
> - Jack Welch, former CEO of General Electric

> "If you spend more time asking appropriate questions rather than giving answers or opinions, your listening [and communication] skills will increase."
> - Bernard Baruch, financier, statesman

What Is A Silo Anyway?

The classic definition of a silo is a tall, cylindrical structure, usually beside a barn, in which fodder is stored. In the jargon of modern war, it is an underground shelter for a missile. In modern behavioral parlance, it can describe the status of a person or a group as being cut off from others. Another meaning is a separate place — either physical or conceptual — where one can go to be alone with one's thoughts.

In business today, we hear that we need to break down silos because they can be counterproductive to organizational success. Now why would we do that, when a silo can provide us with an opportunity to think, create, innovate, and just "be"? Let's look at this silo mentality a little deeper.

If I am someone who needs to think things through on my own, then isn't a silo something I would cherish and naturally create because, quite honestly, I need it to help me be successful? That time alone energizes me and provides an opportunity to conceptualize a plan to achieve success.

The problem with silo thinking arises when we are managers of *people* who need to know what we're thinking so they can do their jobs and do them well. Staying in a self- created silo (while very

PLAYING NICELY WITH OTHERS

comfortable in the short term) could prevent me from making a connection with the very people who will ultimately impact my long-term performance as a leader, as well as the productivity of my team.

If you are a solitary thinker and a leader of people, go into that silo to reenergize your creativity and thinking. However, it is important for you to remember to bring your brain fodder back out and communicate it to the people who need you. It might even be a good idea to discuss your ideas with them to win their buy-in and to ensure you don't have any blind spots in your thinking (which can happen in a silo!).

If you want to be a leader, you must have followers. Good communication is a critical component of every great leader's success. You must identify the best approach for you and your teams. Then implement it with communication, planning, and effort to see the impact it will have. Who knows, you might even become known as a "silo buster"!!!

BREAKDANCING ON A BALANCE BEAM

Winners Hit The Ground Running!

On December 29, 2007, the New England Patriots closed out the year with a record-breaking 16-0 winning season. After winning the first two playoff games, the Patriots became the first professional team since 1884 in any of the four major American sports (football, baseball, basketball and hockey) to win the first 18 games of their season according to the Elias Sports Bureau.

Achieving *goals* is about having them and being flexible with them. In football, as in life, all things have their time and place. While the Patriots lost in the Super Bowl that year (their only loss in an 18-1 season), the day after their big loss, the team had to hit the ground running in order to achieve their new goal of winning in the next season.

This outstanding performance by the Patriots did not happen solely because of Bill Belichick (their coach) or Tom Brady (their quarterback), or Randy Moss (their star wide receiver). It happened because of the quality teamwork that included both visionaries and implementers — those behind the scenes and those in the limelight. The entire team practiced with focus and commitment in order to achieve a goal. Each player knew what he had to do and did it.

PLAYING NICELY WITH OTHERS

This sustained excellence didn't just happen for the Patriots. They spent years building a quality team, measuring and learning from their successes and failures along the way. It took continuous planning, adjustment, communication, teamwork, and leadership for it all to come together... as well as some luck. It took the effort and commitment of each player on that team to make their vision a reality: Wannabes *have* a vision; champions *become* their vision.

"Luck" occurs when preparation meets opportunity. When the dynamics and commitment are present, the value of diversity is recognized so that the whole is greater than the sum of its parts. At that point, great things can happen.

At the start of a new year, or of any new endeavor, as *you* hit the ground running, remember that there are people who need you and are counting on *you* to make it your best year ever — both for yourself and for them! If you set the example by giving your best, you have the right to expect the same from your teammates. Enjoy the ride and celebrate your successes along the way.

Playing Nicely With Others

What happens when you have no choice - you have to play with someone you just can't stand? Is it possible they march to the beat of a different drummer than you do and that you are meant to learn something from them that will help you grow as a person and
Play Nicely With Others?

PLAYING NICELY WITH OTHERS

STEPPING UP
TO THE PLATE

Being held accountable sounds like a very scary thing. And it certainly can be. But except for when we are tiny babies, there comes a time in our lives where we are all held accountable for our actions.

This set of reflections is all about seeking personal accountability and responsibility. It's also about the value of doing so and about why accountability and responsibility are key building blocks for personal growth. So as you read through this next section, keep your eye on the ball and set your personal goal far over the outfield wall. It's all about stepping up to the plate

BREAKDANCING ON A BALANCE BEAM

It's All About Trust

The foundation for a quality organization with successful teams is made of building blocks with a key one being "Trust." The word "trust" can mean different things to people depending on who they are, where they've lived, how they've grown up and their life experiences. Recently, I reached out to individuals of different ages to ask their thoughts about trust. Here are some of their observations:

A 9-year old boy's practical approach: *People are worthy of my trust when they borrow something from me, take care of it and then give it back. If they break it, then I expect them to buy me a new one. If they won't buy me a new one, I will never lend them anything again.*

An 11-year old girl's social approach (with insights that have great applicability to teams): *I trust people when I can believe them and they listen to me; they don't lie to me; and they are really there for me. They break my trust when: they lie to me; they are mean to me; they do not care about what I say — they don't listen; they ignore me.*

A 17-year old young woman's response: *Trust is knowing that another person will always respect and honor you as an* *individual. You respect that person's judgment and know you have the support of that person. I really trust someone who, when part of my team, does what's required and is also there for other people on the team when needed — they share the sense of responsibility and team membership that everyone respects.*

When someone breaks that trust on a team, they have to work to earn it back. They foul up the team dynamics because it's much harder to give them things to do when you don't trust it will be done on time and/or correctly; you always have to verify they did what they were expected to do; you no longer believe that person respects the collegiality of the team and hence it's much harder for the other team members to interact with that person.

Two Gen Xers (ages 27 & 43) responses: *Trust is absolute certainty that you can be yourself without being judged; being open and honest in putting forth your ideas and knowing you will not be critiqued but only the content of your ideas. When trust is broken, that person would have to work harder than everyone else in order to earn back that trust; breaking trust within a team can cause dysfunctionality for the whole team and, potentially, cause it to fail.*

Baby Boomer Responses (ages 50 & 62): *Trust must be earned through shared experiences over time. You enjoy working with people you know and trust. Perhaps this makes it harder for new people to break into the group and makes Boomers look insular and old fashioned. When trust is broken, I feel angered at first and then need to step back and look at the overall situation (practical approach of age) and decide if the relationship is valuable enough to pursue further remediation. This is a setback that can impact the entire team's deliverables. I would have to say something (given their seniority, Boomers tend to be in positions of responsibility) — and that would take some courage on my part — to assure that the issue was dealt with for the overall success of the team.*

So what can we learn from this non-scientific sampling? Perhaps that trust is an essential component of human relationships — whether present or absent. As can be seen, it is given freely when we are young. With life experiences of broken trusts, trust becomes a relationship component which has to be earned over time through shared experience.

BREAKDANCING ON A BALANCE BEAM

In government relationships, countries tend to follow President Reagan's maxim: "Trust, but verify." In business, trust is an essential element for success. It is the grease on the wheels of commerce. Without it, the system would freeze up. When it is breached, there can be serious repercussions including destruction of the business relationship which may have taken years or decades to build.

In daily life, trust can enrich and strengthen human relationships and a lack of it can destroy them. Trust requires work and thought and must be earned every day. When it is present, life is richer. When it is absent, life can be lonely and bleak.

We must always be open to establishing relationships of trust, no matter how often we have been disappointed or hurt in the past. To live a life without trust or the possibility of trust would be a sad existence.

My thanks to all of you for trusting me enough to read this. May you all experience the benefits of trusting relationships in all aspects of your lives!

STEPPING UP TO THE PLATE

Accountability

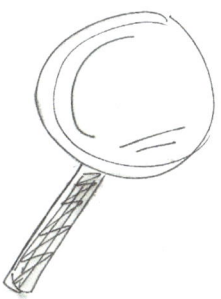

In both our business and personal lives, we are held accountable for our actions. However, what is most important is the level to which we hold ourselves accountable. Here is my definition of accountability:

A Accept "response-ability" for your actions

C Count on your courage and strength of character to pull you through

C Call the shots as you see them

O Open your heart and mind to the ideas and opinions of others

U Understand you are human and know that mistakes will happen

N No blaming, excuses or whining

T Teach others by your example

BREAKDANCING ON A BALANCE BEAM

A Admit when you are wrong

B Be who you are

I Integrity in all that you do

L Listen to learn and understand

I Imitation is the highest form of praise

T Trust yourself

Y Yield to the truth even when it is proclaimed by others

What Is Personal Accountability?

Personal accountability is the willingness to accept responsibility for one's actions or inactions. Accountability exists at all levels, but it is important to make it a part of our everyday lives. Without a daily focus on our goals, it is easy to lose sight of them. Many of us ask "victim" questions:

- Why do I have to do everything?
- When are they going to provide me with more help?
- Why does this always happen to me?
- When is someone going to give me a break?
- When are they going to fix this problem?

These questions imply that someone else is responsible for the problem and for coming up with a solution. What happened to personal accountability? Practice turning blame and victim thinking into personal accountability. You will feel empowered.

A victim mentality is the result of feeling frustrated and overwhelmed. However, that frustration also offers tremendous opportunities to contribute, if we take advantage of them. John Miller, author of The Question Behind the Question, argues that we can make better choices by asking different, more personally accountable "I" questions rather than the victim-like "they" questions. For example:

What can I do to increase my personal productivity?

- How can I make a difference?
- What can I do to help the team?
- What can I do to develop new skills?
- What can I do to support our organization's missions
- How can I do my best at this task?

There is a direct link between commitment to excellence and reward. Success is not the result of luck or good looks; rather, it is the result of a genuine desire to learn, grow and change. We may receive monetary rewards and promotions from faithfully executing a winning attitude. However, the true reward comes from the personal satisfaction we feel for taking control of our lives by answering such questions as, "How can I serve others?" and "What can I do to contribute?"

This chaotic world we live in is the hand we have been dealt; every generation must find a way to "play its hand" to achieve the best result. We cannot control the people with whom we interact and the situations that arise, but we can control our response to them. Make it a personally accountable response and life will be its own reward!

> "If you are to be, you must begin by assuming responsibility.
> You alone are responsible for every moment of your life,
> for every one of your acts."
> - Antoine de Saint-Exupéry in Airman's Odyssey

The Essence Of Style

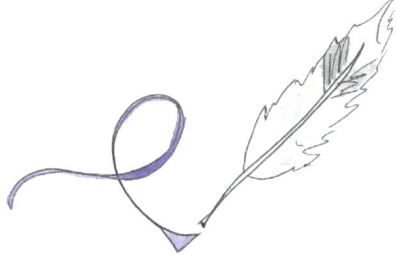

A person's style is the essence of who they are! Many aspects of today's society can minimize the true self and prevent it from shining through. Our teachers — most well-intentioned, some not — provide us with both new and old thoughts, some creative and some staid that, hopefully, will lead us to think for ourselves. The key for each of us lies in the weight we give to what is said or taught so we develop our own style.

Style is unique. To achieve what we were meant to be on this earth, we must constantly strive to pick and choose what works for us, even if it means going against the popular choice. Those times can be trying but, in retrospect, they are the critical ones — the character shapers that are often the turning points for achieving the fullness of our potential. Follow Shakespeare's advice in all areas of your life: "To thine own self be true."

Following are some reflections on the elements of style (not those of Strunk & White, but our own personal style). Life is not a dress rehearsal. It is no deposit, no return. And it's up to us to make our life's dream a reality — in finding the style that belongs to each of us and us alone! Only then will we achieve peace and fulfillment.

"Psychology is action, not thinking about oneself. We continue to shape our personality all our life. To know oneself, one should assert oneself."
— Albert Camus

"We should take care not to make the intellect our god; it has, of course, powerful muscles, but no personality. It has great power but very little compassion."
— Albert Einstein

"Man's main task in life is to give birth to himself,
to become what he potentially is.
The most important product of his effort is his own personality."
— Erich Fromm

"We are free when our actions emanate from our total personality, when they express it, when they resemble it
in the indefinable way a work of art does the artist."
— Henri Bergson

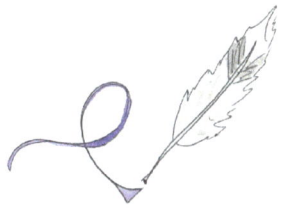

Redefining That Competitive Edge

The other day I was driving with a few young children in the car. They were laughing and talking, all the while each was playing on his Game Boy™. They were playing the same game, looking over each other's shoulders to see who was winning. The click of the keys could be heard as well as their sighs of impatience to be the first one to win the game. Suddenly, a voice cried out from the back of the car: "I Won!" The others started yelling, "Let's do it again!"

When we compete, we draw on our will and perseverance to try again so that the next win can be ours! Sometimes when we compete with one another, the pace of the game helps us achieve that winning goal. At other times, to ensure our future success we need to sit back and reevaluate who we are and how we need to improve to win the game. The quick wins are always fun. However, the win that is achieved through setting a goal and working toward it over the long term is often the most satisfying victory. Through discipline and a positive attitude, we can achieve what others may have thought impossible.

STEPPING UP TO THE PLATE

In our current business environment, many companies are experiencing a competitive advantage; others are losing market share. In both cases, there are opportunities to improve performance.

The companies that are suffering in this economy should be stepping back and reevaluating their business as a whole: What will give them a competitive edge during these tough times? What is a competitive edge? It is an advantage over competitors, whether in athletics, academics or business. No matter how strong a company's standing in the marketplace, it must always look to enhance its competitive edge. In these changing economic times, there may be an even greater opportunity, as well as need, to focus on finding, developing or strengthening our competitive edge.

We have seen some unfortunate examples in recent years of how not to gain a competitive edge, for example, athletes using performance-enhancing drugs. The lesson? Whatever we do to gain a competitive edge must be legal, ethical, positive, and real. Do we really improve our self-confidence, self-esteem or skills (whether in business, academics or sports) by using artificial, external means? If we pursue that route, then the competitive edge is not ours but can be purchased by anyone.

How do we build a real competitive advantage personally or in business? Rather than working furiously at doing what we have always done, we need to assess our current status in light of the challenges and changing conditions. We need to take a step back and ask ourselves the following questions:

- What are our customers' current needs in these changed conditions?
- How can we fill those needs?
- How can we improve our customer service for clients?
- Are we communicating clearly how our services and products are even more valuable in solving the new challenges of these changed times?
- How can we find new clients?

The bottom line for any personal or business competition ultimately lies in the competitor's drive and determination. When times

BREAKDANCING ON A BALANCE BEAM

change, the methods for sales and service success that worked in the past may no longer work. Without sales and quality customer service, companies will fail. There will be situations where a nurturing, customer-focused salesperson can succeed. There will be times when a hard-driving risk-taker is the person needed to innovate and bring in new business. It is essential for companies to determine whether they have the right people in the right jobs (aligned with customer needs and company goals) and to give those employees the needed tools to ensure their success.

The competitive edge is there if we take the time to look within, to turn weaknesses into strengths. We need to look out at the changed landscape and figure out what our customers and potential customers need to be successful and then provide it.

Tee It Up!

When professional golfers compete in tournaments, they "tee it up" to win and be the best that they can be in their profession. When winning eludes them, their focus must shift to improving their game in preparation for the next event.

When we watch professional golfers consistently excel, we realize it's because they have found something they are passionate about and are, on a daily basis, working to perfect. Will they win every time? No. But if they (or, we, for that matter) don't strive to improve, how would they truly understand and appreciate a "win" when they achieve it? Many of us spend so much time on the worry and fear side of life that we miss the fun, stimulation and growth that competition — both winning and losing — can provide.

> "Make sure our attitude determines the way we compete; never let the way we compete determine our attitude."
> - Anonymous

So what better time than now to go for the gold!!! Now is the time to rededicate ourselves to achieving excellence in our personal goals and pursuits. We may not be professional athletes, but we

BREAKDANCING ON A BALANCE BEAM

are all human beings going through this game of life but once. It behooves us to compete and play the game as well as we can. Each of us must learn the rules and keep score on how we are doing in our life game.

It's the fun and passion for life — not the worry and fear of failure — that will help us seize the day and realize our full potential.

"It's never too late to be what you might have been."

- George Eliot

Coaching For The Ages

As a business owner and entrepreneur, I've learned over the years how important it is to hire the right people for the right jobs and, like most of us, I've made many mistakes along the way. I have also learned how important it is to "retain" those "right" people and keep them motivated to learn, grow and develop their skills both within their current roles and for those they aspire to.

Accountability for stoking this motivation and desire rests with both the "employees" and their managers. It's a joint effort — a team sport. However, whether it is a two-person team or 30-person team, the manager (coach) is a critical make or break link to the success — present and future — of each person on the team. Some of you may be thinking: " What? I don't know how to coach. " If you're a manager of people, now may be the time to take a personal inventory of your own strengths and weaknesses so you can better understand your own style and approach. Then you can focus on your strengths and use them to your advantage by "adapting" your style to those being coached.

BREAKDANCING ON A BALANCE BEAM

COACHES need to:

C Communicate their approach and individualize it for each team member.

O Open their minds and offer support when the diligent players fail thus enabling them to rise again by focusing on their development and how they performed rather than the results or outcomes they achieved.

A Adapt their style to engender trust in the coaching relationship which leads to higher levels of commitment and performance.

C Consider carefully each person being coached to identify the leaders and role models to whom the rest of the team will respond positively.

H Help those being coached to achieve their dreams in a positive, passionate way.

If a coach does all this well, s/he will be a positive role model and a key ingredient in the success of the team. They will all "win together" — the number on the scoreboard may not always show it. But, as they grow to respect and understand one another, the numbers will change and the team will win!!

> "What we have done for ourselves alone dies with us; what we have done for others and the world remains and is immortal."
>
> – Albert Pike

Contemplating Courage

I received the following email written by someone for whom I have the utmost respect and regard. I think this captures worthwhile ideas and topics for all of us to ponder. I hope you enjoy it and take time to think about the points made.

****

The wake-up call came at 6am. I grappled with the phone and then fumbled to grab hold of my glasses and turn on the TV.

More people died in bombings today, our soldiers were on high alert in the Middle East, and the airport screening process here in the U.S. was adding to travel times.

I got out of bed, put my running shoes on and headed out of the hotel.

I ran past the White House and thought of all the great patriots who have resided there. Regardless of political ideology, the post of Commander-in-Chief is unbelievably burdensome and demands tremendous self-sacrifice.

BREAKDANCING ON A BALANCE BEAM

I ran up the steps of the Lincoln Memorial and — pausing at the top out of respect — considered the supreme sacrifice made by President Lincoln and the courage he exhibited during this country's Civil War.

I ran past the war monuments — Vietnam, Korea and WWII — and was overwhelmed as I contemplated the unselfish acts of sacrifice by those who served in these wars. Members of my own family have served during war time, and I am grateful for their sacrifices...but they had a connection to me — or at least the prospect of me. The incomprehensible sacrifice is that of the people who did not know me, who would never know me. They were from different walks of life than me, had different interests and different political ideologies than me. Indeed, they would never have reason to cross paths with me or my family members. Yet they risked — and many gave — their lives to protect my freedom, my way of life. How do you show gratitude for that kind of courage? How do you thank the faceless soldiers who sacrificed so much?

I ran past the Washington monument and reflected upon the wisdom and courage of the Father of our Nation. His larger than life persona and willingness to forego a role as King — which many wanted him to take — for one as President, evidenced a principled ethic and leadership rarely seen today.

I ran to the base of the Capitol. I could not go up the steps because terrorists have altered our security procedures. As I stared at this magnificent building, the weight of the matters debated and decided there was almost palpable. Many great leaders have passionately advocated for their beliefs and constituencies in this house of our representative democracy.

At the end of my run, the conclusion was inescapable — we are so very privileged to live in the greatest country on earth. So many sacrificed so much to provide us with the freedoms we all too often take for granted. We are an irrepressibly optimistic people and, while terrorists may change our procedures and our plans, they will never change our spirit.

This nation and its people are great not because of things we have built or wars we have fought, but because we are evidence that freedom and democracy are the most noble of pursuits.

STEPPING UP TO THE PLATE

And while these buildings, monuments and statues do not - in and of themselves — make us great, they do something far more important. They give testimony to the magnitude of the sacrifices made by so many...for people they would never know. That is true courage.

I am so grateful for being able to take this run today — for the freedom to do so, and for the reminders of greatness that I encountered.

I humbly thank all those who sacrificed on my behalf. I am more grateful than I could ever express for the gift of freedom I have been given and for the opportunity to see my children grow up with this same gift.

God Bless America.

Stepping Up To The Plate

We must all be accountable for our actions, at home and work, but it's not always easy or comfortable. Why is *Stepping Up To The Plate* often scary and difficult to do?

STEPPING UP TO THE PLATE

HANGING IN THERE

In spite of our best efforts to organize, chaos happens. And sometimes it happens a lot. What do you do when chaos happens so frequently that it seems to become the norm? If you're like me, you try really hard to figure out a way to just hang in there long enough to come up with a plan to deal with it.

This set of musings is the result of many years of hanging in there — sometimes by my fingernails — and, as such, covers a number of ideas about just what each of us can do to cope with those unexpected curve balls that business, and life in general, throw at us. These things have worked for me and have taught me a lot.

BREAKDANCING ON A BALANCE BEAM

In The Black

A number of years ago, when my son was seven, he asked me to buy him a game for his computer. I told him I didn't have the money to buy it for him. He looked at me like I was clueless and said, "Just go to the bank and get some money from the machine." In the eyes of a child, getting what you want is just that simple and logical — go to the ATM and it will give you money! If only it were that easy.

How often do we find ourselves falling short of cash, energy, enthusiasm, ideas, determination, inspiration, joy or solutions to our problems? If we could only go to a machine and get what we need, it would be a wonderful world.

Why are we so often "in the red?" The speed of doing business has never been faster. With Blackberries™, iPhones™, iPads™, email, voicemail, cell phones, and texting, we are always open for business. There is no excuse for being unreachable in today's business world. Yet, if we keep making withdrawals from our personal account, we are bound to end up in the red by incurring deficits like insomnia, stress, ulcers, anger, or fatigue.

HANGING IN THERE

How to stay "in the black." Keeping ourselves "in the black" takes awareness and conscious effort. Here are some sources for deposits to your "account":

- Surround yourself with positive people. Find people in your life who have the positive energy to give you a jump start when your battery is weak. Instead of sucking energy from you with negativity, these people energize you. Reach out to them when you need a boost.

- Read an inspirational book. Reading about how other people have overcome obstacles and challenges or took a unique approach to life can help you view your own challenges from a different perspective.

- Unplug yourself. Make a point of turning off your cell phone, Blackberry™, iPhone™, or email for a period of time each day or week. Giving yourself some quiet, uninterrupted time on a regular basis frees your mind to sort through the data it's already processing, allowing you to work more effectively. You will discover that these unplugged times give you an amazing return on investment.

- Study something of interest. Take that course on organic gardening. Read a book about ancient Egyptian civilization. Enroll with your dog in Therapy Dog training so you can take him to nursing homes and hospitals to bring joy to others.

- Exercise your body. Yoga, walking, breakdancing, Pilates, swimming — any form of exercise releases endorphins that make huge deposits to your personal energy account.

Remember, even the ATM shuts down for maintenance. Be sure to give yourself some down time to stay "in the black" for the long term.

Count Me In

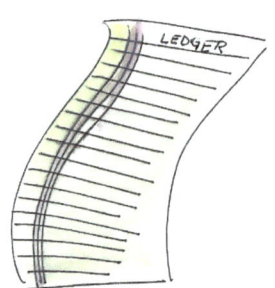

As a CPA and owner of a business, I'm all too familiar with assets and liabilities, profit and loss, balance sheets, and cash flows. These terms speak to the viability, or lack thereof, of a business. I recently read an article that applied these accounting terms to *people*. On the P&L, people are an expense item — salaries, taxes, development, dues, and subscriptions. But any business owner, executive, or manager knows those same people are an organization's most important *asset*! To borrow a phrase from Gilbert and Sullivan's *The Pirates of Penzance*, this seems to be "a paradox, a paradox, a most ingenious paradox!" Why are people counted on the expense side of the business when, without them, there would *be* no business?

According to Kathryn Cramer, co-author of *Change the Way You See Everything*, if we business people want to improve our bottom line, it is in our best interest to move from "deficit-based thinking" to "asset-based thinking" regarding our people. However, bottom-line people results do not just happen. It takes planning and hard work to hire, develop, and retain talent. And, beyond that, it takes a lot of *perseverance* to create a successful human capital management program. The following quotes highlight the importance of perseverance and courage in achieving great things — in all aspects of life-including this one:

HANGING IN THERE

"The question isn't who is going to let me; it's who is going to stop me."
                - Ayn Rand, *The Fountainhead*

"Most of the things worth doing in the world had been declared impossible before they were done."
                - Louis L. Brandeis,
                Supreme Court Justice

"Only those who risk going too far can possibly find out how far one can go."
                - T. S. Eliot

"Many of life's failures are people who did not realize how close they were to success when they gave up."
                - Thomas Edison

"You gain strength, courage, and confidence by every experience in which you really stop to look fear in the face. You must do the thing which you think you cannot do."
                - Eleanor Roosevelt

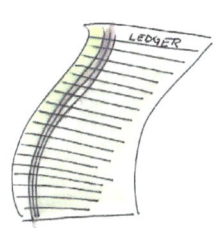

Take A Look Inside

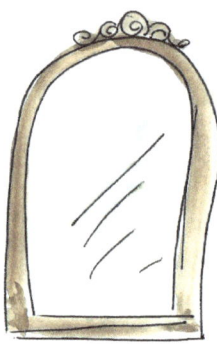

"The unexamined life is not worth living."
- Socrates

If you look within yourself, you may be pleasantly surprised at what you find! Things are not always what they seem. Oftentimes we make quick judgments about people. In fact, studies show that first impressions are often lasting ones. But, in reality, those first (and sometimes last!!) impressions may not be accurate. Our own perception of the event may cloud the reality about others and, as a result, we may overlook seeing that diamond in the rough!

How about the first impressions we have of ourselves? Taking an honest look inside is the first step toward gaining a true picture of how others see us. And yet, how often do we take the time to look — really look — at ourselves and understand who we really are? Sometimes what we see can frighten us, especially if we've been running away or avoiding a difficult issue. Or maybe — just maybe — what we see could be awesome, providing us with a solid platform for opportunities and adventures.

HANGING IN THERE

It's the examination of life that allows us to understand our purpose. People may appear to be complex, but in reality we are simple — we just try to make ourselves complex, perhaps to prevent confronting reality. We often put up walls and barriers that appear in our mind's eye to be insurmountable. And, yet, if we just sit down and listen (that "take a break" idea!), we will find a lot of the answers. At that point, we can begin to build bridges instead of walls.

Life is short, and time is fleeting — yet both are full of opportunity! In our stress-filled, frenetic world, we often don't take the time to learn about the most important person in the world — *ourself*. Who would you prefer to be with: Someone who understands who they are and makes the most of it, or someone who is running scared and won't listen to options or new approaches?

A daily mini-vacation is something few of us take, but it's a break from which we can all benefit. The quiet mind brings calm and with it answers to our questions about who we are and where we want to go. Looking inside ourselves can make all the difference in how we relate to the people in our lives — but most importantly, to *ourselves*.

When we reach the end of our days, it will hopefully become clear to us what is truly important about life: It's not the things we've accumulated or the money we have in the bank; what is truly important are the people in our lives and what we have done with our time on earth.

> "We must be the change we wish to see in the world."
> - M.K. Gandhi

BREAKDANCING ON A BALANCE BEAM

"Got No Checkbooks, Got No Banks"

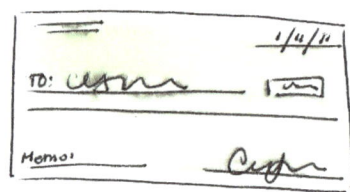

"Got no checkbooks, got no banks.
Still I'd like to express my thanks —
I got the sun in the morning and the moon at night."
- Irving Berlin, from
Annie Get Your Gun

At the age of 8, upon the death of his father, Irving Berlin quit school and sold newspapers to help support his family. He also performed in public for tips and gratuities. The lyrics above impart Berlin's message that, despite difficult circumstances, there are always things in life to be thankful for — things that money cannot buy and that are free for the taking; things that are simple, majestic and beautiful that we take for granted (and, therefore, overlook) every day!

The current worldwide economic crisis will continue to impact the way we view money, investments, and financial institutions — and our lifestyles. The future is unclear, but in the meantime, we must live our lives to the fullest. Difficult times and experiences teach us many of life's valuable lessons. We may not realize the value of the lessons as we are experiencing them; but, in retrospect, when we have time to reflect, we will always discover new insights. It is the way we are wired as human beings.

HANGING IN THERE

One thing is certain, even in perilous times — our attitude will determine our altitude. We can all benefit from Berlin's wonderful attitude during his time of difficulty, and to quote Robert Quillen, "count all of our assets [including 'the sun in the mornin' and the moon at night'] and we will always show a profit."

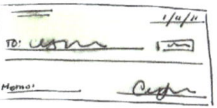

BREAKDANCING ON A BALANCE BEAM

A Painted Sky

One fall evening in Florida, as I sat overlooking the intra-coastal waterway with the sun setting at the edge of the horizon, the sky was at once brilliantly blue, orange, pink and gray. The simple majesty of the scene reminded me that beauty like this needs to be appreciated at every opportunity. And now, I thought it might be worth a moment (or two) to reflect on the beautiful things that life offers all of us and, amazingly, a lot of them are "free".

The practical demands of life — professional, the job, schoolwork, homework, busywork — will always be with us. They are all good and necessary for, in many ways, work does make us grow, learn and contribute to society. But, in all that effort, many quiet moments that we could enjoy get passed by because we're too busy and don't have the time — or don't make the time — to savor them.

I was recently reading the book, <u>Life On Purpose</u>, by Brad Swift. In it, he cited a quote by Mark Twain which helped me take notice of that *painted sky*:

> "Twenty years from now you will be more disappointed by the things that you didn't do than by the ones you did do. So throw off the bowlines. Sail away from the safe harbor. Catch the trade winds in your sails."

> *Explore. Dream. Discover.*

HANGING IN THERE

It's the little things in life that, in the end, make a big difference in the quality of our lives: the innocence and creativity of children; heartfelt laughter; simple beauty; the exercise of freedom; the love of family; the good fellowship and support of friends — to name a few.

Now that I am trying harder to listen and observe these moments, I paused as I was putting two little ones to sleep a few weeks ago. After I read them a story, they asked me to sing them three songs — they didn't care which three and they clearly didn't care about my lack of singing ability. When I got to the last song, I told them I was now going to sing them my "Signature Song." I asked if they knew what that was and, in unison, they said: "Let there be Peace On Earth and Let It Begin With Me."

In closing, may peace, love and joy be with all of you so you may enjoy the simple beauties of life.

Hanging In There

*We all have our days, weeks or months when life throws us curve balls we didn't expect.
In this moment in time, how can we dig down deep to find the courage and strength to just Hang In There?*

HANGING IN THERE

BEING OPEN TO CHANGE

What is it about change that makes us dig in our heels and resist it with every fiber of our being? What are we afraid of? What might happen if we took all the passion we put into resisting change and embraced it instead? After all, isn't life changing every day anyway?

Why do we waste so much energy trying to stop or fight change?

Embracing Change

Despite the constant change that impacts our lives, there are some things in life that just don't change! Each of us needs to find the right balance between the forces of change and the constants in life that provide us with a sense of security — that give us a richer life and a sense of purpose to our days.

We have a choice. The following thoughts may help you to accept and work with change to bring balance into your life.

> "Carpe Diem!"(Sieze The Day!")
> - Horace, Roman Poet, 68 B.C.- 8 B.C

- We go to sleep each night and wake up every morning to a new day full of adventure and opportunity.

- We can choose to make a difference to others or watch the world go by.

- We can dream and create a life that is all our own, or we can sit back and just let life happen to us.

- The shortest distance between despair and hope is a good night's sleep.

- Children develop ideas and concepts that are different from the generation before them. It is part of the human condition called *progress*.

BEING OPEN TO CHANGE

- Each of us is a unique being. If we do not contribute our uniqueness to the world and thereby change it, no one else can.

- Truly listening to others gives us a different perspective that can open up whole new vistas.

- As we age, we trade youth for wisdom and experience and the chance to love and be loved.

> "Every day is a fresh beginning;
> each morn is the world made new."
> - Sarah Chauncey Woolsey

Change happens, whether we like it or not. You can seize it, go with it, create it...or fight it! The choice is yours.

Opportunities Versus Obstacles

Recently, I was in a meeting with the CEO of a client company discussing a business issue. He listened to me, sat back in his chair, and then said, "Kathy, for someone who is always upbeat and positive, you are looking at a lot of things lately as obstacles. You need to turn those obstacles into opportunities because that's what successful people do! And, the only way to do that is to change your thinking and look to the countless possibilities surrounding each obstacle — one step at a time." His words meant a lot to me. They were that "swift kick" all of us need from time to time to move us to higher ground.

At the 2008 US Open golf tournament, Tiger Woods demonstrated how, despite his knee injury, he focused on the opportunity that lay ahead of him — another US Open title. He could have withdrawn, but chose not to. Instead, he focused his undivided attention on the Torrey Pines golf course and his golf game. He was not competing against the field or even his playoff opponent, Rocco Mediate. Mediate was addressing his own challenge of coming back, at age 45, from years without victory. Both athletes were competing with themselves for an opportunity that was important to them.

BEING OPEN TO CHANGE

People in the gallery cheered for both players, encouraging and supporting them in achieving their dreams. Neither failed; they gave the game their best efforts to take advantage of the opportunity they both worked so hard to achieve. It is less important where they finished than that they gave their all as a magnificent example of full commitment to attaining a goal.

The important lesson to take away is that if we never try to earn the opportunities and just complain about the obstacles, then life and all it has to offer will pass us by.

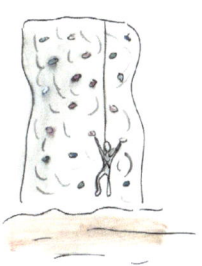

The Art Of Selling Change

> "All is connected. No one thing can change by itself."
> - Paul Hawken, *Natural Capitalism*

Frito Lay™ has a popular product on the market called Smart Food®. Ken Meyers, one of the original developers of Smart Food, remarked:

> "I don't care who you are or what you do, but each of you in this room is a salesperson — whether you like it or not. You're selling to both your external and internal customers. And in order for people to change their way of thinking and buy what you're selling, it is imperative that you listen with understanding to what they want and give it to them!"

Too often, we are so set in our thinking that we "tell" rather than "sell" to our prospective purchasers. We fail to really listen to their concerns and wants. We need to take the time to understand what motivates them to "buy into" a new way of doing things. If we don't don the hat of the salesperson, we will lose the sale and be forced to try implementing change on unwilling customers!!

People frequently resist change because no one has taken the time to communicate with them and help them understand how the change will happen and what its impact will be. People who

BEING OPEN TO CHANGE

are treated with respect for their intelligence and work ethic often surprise leaders with their ability to implement a successful change process. Companies pay for the minds and expertise of their employees. Employees will throw in their hearts and souls for free when they are motivated to participate in a common cause that benefits them.

Communication and planning helps transition from the old to the new, and from the established way of doing things to the new and improved approach. To create successful organizational change, it is important to "walk a mile in the shoes" of the implementers — the customers of the change process. Listen to their concerns, ideas, and thoughts. Question them directly to identify their needs and provide them with the best scenario for change. Then close the deal by helping them implement the change. The sales process ends when the customer "buys" the change. The next phase is customer service — when the implementers are supported and reinforced in their efforts.

So you see, to successfully implement change, we must all be salespeople whether we like it or not. The key is to understand what people are concerned about and what they need (want) to succeed in the change.

> "Consider how hard it is to change yourself, and you'll understand what little chance you have of trying to change others."
> – Jacob Braude.

Out-Of-The-Box Thinkers

We Need Them, But Do We Really Want Them? Out-of-the box thinking and innovation are hallmarks of successful companies around the globe. Changing market conditions, trends, and competition require companies to adapt for continued success. With success comes growth and the need for formal structure, processes, and controls — which can stifle change and innovation. The dilemma is how to balance innovation and change with the organization's need for consistent quality implementation and execution.

What is a leader to do when faced with a culture that is moving away from innovation and inventiveness and moving toward familiarity and the status quo? One answer is to get some out-of-the-box thinkers on board. These are people who have a willingness to bring new and innovative perspectives to the day-to-day work environment. They have no problem doing things differently, and doing different things. Problem fixed, right? Well, not exactly.

The good news first: Getting out-of-the-box thinkers onboard isn't as difficult as it might appear. Now the bad news: There is more to it than just hiring or promoting out-of-the-box thinkers.

BEING OPEN TO CHANGE

To save your company from the world of status quo, you must ensure that the right foundation is in place. That is, the organization must commit to welcome and support innovators and change agents. Innovative cultures require at least some of their people to seek new opportunities, accept risk and change, and work cross-functionally. Innovative companies require their leaders across-the-board to create the right environments to guide and promote inventive behavior. Innovative cultures even have a performance appraisal and reward system that supports trial-and-error attempts at being creative!

Understand that although creativity and innovation can be the lifeblood of an organization, not every person in the company should be a change agent; otherwise, chaos would ensue. Creative thinkers are critical for success, but it is also critical that their contributions be integrated appropriately through a behaviorally diverse and balanced workforce. Change agents are the leavening in the bread, not the entire loaf. A clever business leader seeks to place these change agents in atmospheres where they can flourish and feel appreciated, while staying within the boundaries and culture of the overall organization.

Being Open To Change

"Every day is a fresh beginning; and each morn is the world made new." Change is always with us. So why is it that Change is something we often resist? What might happen if we put more effort into
Being Open To Change
than resisting it?

BEING OPEN TO CHANGE

COMMUNICATING EFFECTIVELY

How many times have you had a problem communicating with someone? Communicating the old-fashioned way (speaking face-to-face with someone) is difficult enough, but to complicate things further, technology provides a myriad of ways to do it: email using whole words and, sometimes, complete sentences; texting using keywords, abbreviations and acronyms; code that uses dashes and dots/long and short bursts of noise — Yikes!!

On the balance beam of life, being able to communicate effectively is like having an extra support mechanism — a tool that helps us find a center of equilibrium in our interactions. When we mess it up, oftentimes it makes whatever is supposed to happen next not happen — at least in the way we had hoped.

It is vital to become aware of how we communicate — and what happens when we fail to do it well. In the name of good communication, I invite your own thoughts and comments.

The Medium Is The Message...Or Is It?

What happens when that message is always email? Are we in email overdrive? Remember when the words "You've got mail" were new, different, and exciting? We were all so enamored by this unique communication approach and couldn't wait to use it. The age of technology was opening another chapter that brought intrigue and adventure into our lives and — best of all — it was quick, easy, and global! It enabled us to reach people across time zones and those we could just never get on the telephone!

But what happens when the intrigue and adventure of email starts to wear off and we are getting 30, 40, 50 emails a day? Have emails become so routine that other forms of communication in the workplace are thrown off balance? Add to that, instant messaging and text messaging and now we have an electronic information blizzard of epic proportion!

Have these constantly increasing methods of communication led us to a shortage of face-to-face verbal interaction and the natural human connection? Where are we headed? What have we become?

During a recent interview, renowned primatologist Jane Goodall commented on emails:

"Email can be the most dangerous form of communication because of its peculiar character: email "compels" the recipient to send an answer immediately and, with usually a huge number of emails waiting in our inbox, we frequently end up saying things we wouldn't say in person or on the phone."

Our innate personality style — the human side of each of us — often shows up immediately without the opportunity for personal interaction with our intended recipients to clarify any misunderstandings or fill in any lack of context. We respond to emails based on our own perception, our own frame of reference and our personality biases. Add emotion, stress, impulse and temper to that mix and we may respond now and regret later!

Are we as a society out of whack in our communications? Like everything in life, it is a balancing act. Some of us prefer e-mail; others face-to-face communication. But weren't we born to want and need each other both physically and mentally? And yet we also know that new technology is not going away. In places like Microsoft, according to NFO CM Research Ltd., "email has become the pervasive communication medium...where probably 99% of communication takes place via email...and the phone never rings."

According to the Media Richness Theory, first proposed in 1984 by Richard L. Daft and Robert H. Lengel:

> "The greater the likelihood of a message being misinterpreted, the greater the need for rich media. The theory suggests that choosing a medium which matches the task is likely to lead to the most effective outcome."

But more information does not mean better information! Think before you react to an email. Sometimes it's better to wait or just go and see the person (or give them a call) than to respond right away by email.

BREAKDANCING ON A BALANCE BEAM

Two Tips:

- The medium is the message
- Think twice before pressing that Send button

If you wouldn't say it to someone face-to-face, it's probably a good sign that you should not write it, either!!

Happy emailing!!

COMMUNICATING EFFECTIVELY

Music Speaks Volumes

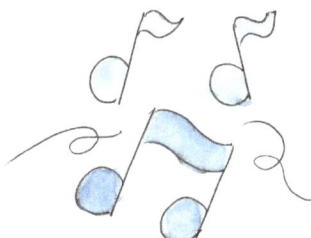

When I was a freshman in college I signed up for my first real music class, thinking it would be simple — like Do-Re-Mi — and I would get an easy A. On my first day of class, however, I was astonished to learn the professor did not hail from my musical planet. He immediately told us we would be asked to write a term paper comparing Paul Hindemith's Mathis der Mahler to Beethoven's 3rd Symphony, the Eroica. A pre-requisite for writing this paper was to attend three live, classical symphonies of our choice and analyze what the music communicated to us. At first I sat there and said "Holy Cow, how am I ever going to do this?" But then, as with anything in life that requires change and growth, I said "I can do this," although I had no idea how!

That course turned out to be one of my most meaningful learning experiences. It taught me how music — if you really listen — speaks to all of us. Some of us like Jazz; for others it's Hard Rock, Reggae, Hip Hop, Classical, Country, New Age or Rock'n Roll. When it stirs our emotions and reaches our inner being, music is an effective form of communication, a true work of art. Indeed, music has been called the language of emotion.

When I attended the three symphonies, the music spoke to me in different ways, and stirred very different emotions. Sometimes it made me happy: Tchaikovsky's 1812 Overture; sometimes

BREAKDANCING ON A BALANCE BEAM

it made me want to dance: Ravel's Bolero; and sometimes it depressed me: Mozart's Requiem. But each piece contained and communicated its own beauty. The real lesson I learned in that course — other than that there is a world of music to experience beyond the current Top Forty Hits — is that music communicates a message from the composer sent through the conductor and musicians to the audience. Whether there is a standing ovation or the audience boos, it teaches a profound lesson in effective communication. The beauty of music lies in the:

- Space between the notes
- Exquisite balance and synchronization of the instruments
- Timing of the conductor and orchestra
- Ability of the conductor and musicians to work together to create beauty

Practice, thought and hard work are the building blocks of a great musical performance conveying emotion, insight, visual images and interpretative opinion — the attributes of communication.

My college professor helped me understand Leonard Bernstein's words, "Music names the unnamable and communicate[s] the unknowable" by stretching my mind to think about music as life and as an art form of communication.

Life is the music that we all make. It is how we manage the high and low notes and how much we commit to making the music powerful, emotional and beautiful that makes all the difference in how our wonderful, unique symphony of life is received by the audience.

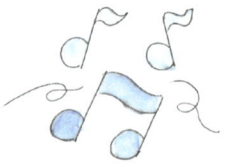

COMMUNICATING EFFECTIVELY

A, B, Triple C

Early in my career, I met with the Chairman of the Board of a NYSE — listed company: That meeting had a powerful impact on my life. He told me that in business and in life you should always follow the KISS rule — Keep It Simple Stupid — as a means to engage and communicate with your audience. Over time, his words continue to ring true — to engage people in the workplace and at home; the key is to connect with your audience in a language they understand. It's really as simple as A, B, Triple C!!!

A   Adaptability

"If you live in the river, you should make friends with the crocodile."
                    - Indian Proverb

To connect with other people, we must be willing to put our egos aside and adapt our natural style by putting ourselves in the shoes of our customers, be they our child, co-worker, colleague or boss.

BREAKDANCING ON A BALANCE BEAM

B   Balance

"A well-developed sense of humor is the pole that adds balance to your step as you walk the tightrope of life."
- William Arthur Ward

Being able to laugh at ourself brings balance and levity to situations, enabling others to see the human side of a person — we all have our moments when we're off balance.

C   Confidence

"Whatever you say, say it with conviction."
- Mark Twain

To sell our message, we need to deliver it with confidence and believe we can impact our audience — especially if we've done the necessary preparation and homework. Don't second-guess yourself.

C   Courage

"Keep your fears to yourself, but share your courage with others."
- Robert Louis Stevenson

Sometimes in business and in our personal life, it is necessary to take a stand even when others do not agree with us. These moments test our spirit but enable us to engage ourselves and stand up for what we believe is right.

C   Civility

"It takes two to speak the truth — one to speak and another to hear."
- Henry David Thoreau

COMMUNICATING EFFECTIVELY

In our world of emails, texting, blogging and virtual offices, our written words oftentimes disengage the reader. At those times it is important to pick up the phone or walk next door to visit our colleagues and show them the civility, professionalism and respect they deserve. Through simple human contact, we can better engage another person and communicate our message with confidence and courage. Face-to-face communication often prevents a battle of empty or misunderstood words.

So life really is as simple as A, B, Triple C:

> "Most of the fundamental ideas of science are essentially simple, and may, as a rule, be expressed in a language comprehensible to everyone.
>
> If the fundamentals of modern science can be expressed simply, surely our everyday lives need to be kept simple, too, for the greatest enjoyment and happiness."
> -Albert Einstein

Are They Really As They Seem?

Myths are traditional, typically ancient, stories featuring supernatural beings or heroes who defy the laws of nature or do things beyond common experience. They frequently served as a worldview of a people to explain naturally occurring phenomena. Myths are a way of explaining and making sense of the world, to make it more manageable.

In the nineteenth and twentieth centuries, myths were replaced by science to provide the explanations needed to understand our world. However, it is one thing to know facts and have scientific insights; it is quite another to understand how people perceive and integrate this knowledge.

Despite how highly we regard our scientific sophistication, we still understand very little about the motivations and actions of people. Typically we rely on our *own* perceptions of the actions and motivations of others to understand and explain them. We may misjudge people — creating our own subjective myths about them — which can impede productivity and progression in life and business. Perhaps these personal myths or judgments that we make are our attempts to explain and make sense of our world, thereby making it manageable. For example, first impressions can be deceiving:

COMMUNICATING EFFECTIVELY

"That person is...

- a snob.
- full of herself.
- so detailed he can't get out of his own way.
- not strategic.
- lacking a sense of humor.
- too wordy.
- too quiet."

Take a closer look at the snap judgments made in these examples. How can we avoid being misled by our own myths — subjective judgments perhaps true, perhaps false — about people? Let's consider some alternative views of the above characterizations:

- A *snob* might just be someone who is shy and uncomfortable in social settings. Because of that, this person may appear aloof or distant to people who are more extroverted.
- People who appear to be *full of themselves* may, in fact, be people who love to verbalize their thinking and ideas, get excited about the world and are open to talking about their own accomplishments and achievements.
- People who are *so detailed they can't get out of their own way* may have a strong need to learn all that they can when moving into new areas or situations, to avoid making a mistake.
- When we say someone is *not strategic*, we may really mean that he does not agree with what we think is important. This may be a flag for us to communicate our view/"sell our plan" in a different way, using a different approach.
- When we say someone *lacks a sense of humor*, we may feel that they do not communicate in a way that makes us laugh or feel happy. However, we all have a sense of humor, although how it manifests itself depends on many variables, such as geography, education, culture, context, maturity and who we are behaviorally.

- When we describe a person as *too wordy*, we are put off by a style of speaking that is perhaps less succinct than our own. However, if we allow ourselves to become distracted by the delivery of the message, we may miss hearing its substance.

- When we perceive someone to be *too quiet*, we may feel that the person is dismissive of, or not engaged in our conversation. However, "still waters run deep" and we may learn a lot from that person, if we are wise enough to plumb the depths.

Human behavior has not changed since ancient times, when myths were created to explain and manage the world. We have made great strides in science and technology but our understanding and management of human behavior remain primitive.

Human nature cannot be reduced to scientific formulas or mathematical equations. We need excitement, spontaneity, creativity and fun in our lives to thrive. We need to continually develop different methods of effective communication as we collaborate with other people to achieve our goals. We need to think beyond the myths we create about people and ensure that we are open to seeing them for all that they are.

Communicating Effectively

Communication is a two-way street. What happens when you're on the same street but going in opposite directions? Why is it that Communicating Effectively can often hit so many road blocks?

BEING ABLE TO LAUGH

Do you know people who take themselves too seriously? Have you gotten into the habit of taking yourself too seriously?

The health benefits of a good old-fashioned belly laugh cannot be overstated. There are many advantages to being able to laugh (especially at yourself) and living your life with an upbeat attitude, especially when you need it the most.

In the spirit of good health and just plain old *fun*, I present to you my thoughts on *Being Able To Laugh*.

Laughing Can Be The Best Treat!

During the holidays, the fun and laughter of kids is all around us! And, if we're lucky, the kid inside each of us may rear its head a little bit, too! Those two simple words, "fun" and "laughter," have the same effect on kids and adults — they put a smile on our faces! And smiles can magically light up a room for young and old alike.

In his recent book, The Difference Maker — Making Your Attitude Your Greatest Asset, John Maxwell quoted several lines from Helen Hayes' autobiography, On Reflection. The legendary actress tells a story about her initial attempt at cooking Thanksgiving dinner. Before serving the meal, she warned her son and husband, "This is the first turkey I've ever cooked. If it isn't any good, I don't want anybody to say a word. We'll just get up from the table, without comment or criticism, and go out to a restaurant to eat." When the meal was prepared and she walked out of the kitchen to put the turkey on the table, she found her husband and son seated there — with their hats and coats on.

Humor can bring levity, insight, and truth to life and business. It teaches us how to not take ourselves too seriously. Laughter is contagious and can quickly spread from person to person. As we

BEING ABLE TO LAUGH

go about our day-to-day activities at work or at play, wouldn't it be great to just have some fun — to lighten up and not worry so much! Laughter is known to boost morale and energy, and takes our minds off the sometimes difficult challenges we face day to day. In a sense, laughing or having fun (or even just putting a smile on our faces), can provide that mini-vacation in our day that can spur us on to achieve great things. It can also help us relax and gain some balance in our daily life which, all too often, is filled with stress, challenges and, yes, opportunities.

Following are some thoughts on laughter and fun, as well as some attempts to make you laugh:

"Laughter is the shortest distance between two people"
- Victor Borge

"The best way to make your audience laugh is to start laughing yourself."
- Oliver Goldsmith, Anglo-Irish Author, Playwright

"The human race has only one effective weapon--and that is laughter."
- Mark Twain

"Any man who has the job I've had and didn't have a sense of humor wouldn't still be here."
- Harry S. Truman

"If you want creative workers, give them enough time to play."
- John Cleese

"If you never have, you should. These things are fun and fun is good."
- Oh, the Places You'll Go, Dr. Seuss

BREAKDANCING ON A BALANCE BEAM

The Value Of A Smile

In this frenetic world, we may find ourselves losing perspective on what's really important. In the scheme of things, our lives are short. And yet it seems many of us are always in a hurry to get things done, rushing around and not having much fun!!! But if we don't take the time to stop, look and listen, our precious life will be over — like a blip on a screen!!!

There are times when we need to slow life down and enjoy some of its simple pleasures. A smile is a simple pleasure that each of us can easily share with others — our loved ones, our business colleagues, our customers and our friends. A smile can have an immediate "return on investment" for you and for those whom you care about.

> "It costs nothing, but creates much.
> It enriches those who receive, without impoverishing those who give.
> It happens in a flash, and the memory of it sometimes lasts forever."
> - The Value of a Smile,
> Frank Irving Fletcher

BEING ABLE TO LAUGH

A special little one named Courtney Elizabeth was in her car seat and every time I turned around to see how she was doing, she would scowl at me! Finally, I gently squeezed her leg and said: "Are you smiling?" She looked at me and scowled even more. I then said, "I know there's a smile in that beautiful face somewhere!! Come on, Ms. Courtney Elizabeth — let me see it! And then a beautiful big smile emerged. That smile lives within each of us. When we give it away to others the world usually smiles back at us. Courtney certainly made my day when she did. And today, 11 years later, whenever she writes to me she always adds: P.S.: I'm smiling!!

BREAKDANCING ON A BALANCE BEAM

Laughter Is The Shortest Distance

Several years ago as I was walking my granddaughter, Bailey, into her 1st grade classroom, we met up with one of her classmates and his Dad. The little boy's Dad said to Bailey, "Is this your Mom?" To which she replied, "No, this is my grandmother." The gentleman looked at me somewhat surprised and said, "Whatever you're doing, keep at it!!!" I started to laugh and said "I'm doing my best!!" I then turned to Bailey and said, "See, he thinks I'm young enough to be your mother!" To which Bailey replied (and put it all in perspective!!): "You're not young; you've got wrinkles." I cracked up laughing and said in reply: "And do you know why I have wrinkles, Ms. Bailey? Because I laugh a lot."

> "Humor is also a way of saying something serious."
> - T. S. Eliot

At work and at home, we all need to reach out and laugh more than we do today. A good belly laugh can lower blood pressure, boost the immune system, reduce stress, improve brain function and reduce the risk of heart disease!

BEING ABLE TO LAUGH

> "A round man cannot be expected to fit in a square hole right away. He must have time to modify his shape."
> - Mark Twain

When I read this quote by Mark Twain, the visual made me laugh and I thought, how appropriate for today's world. At all levels in business today, the "round peg in a square hole" philosophy costs businesses in time and results and has a major impact on their bottom lines. Hiring and promoting people into roles that just don't fit their behavioral style causes individuals to work really hard (and long) at trying to be something they are not. Trying to change one habit, let alone many behaviors, to meet the demands of a job takes time and enormous effort. When the fit isn't there, the cost to the individual and the company can be extraordinary. In the process, that "round man" will get rounder and rounder and will ultimately suffocate the lifeblood of his natural skills and talents, diminishing his self-confidence and self-esteem, and making it difficult for him to be successful.

However, if individuals and organizations are smart (and objective) and look at that "round man/square hole" decision as the wrong paradigm, they can take a much more positive approach by trying to match round with round and square with square! This does not mean that people cannot adapt. However, at the extreme margins there is less flexibility in behavioral styles. As in all of life, as we move to the middle, there is more flexibility and adaptability. The point is that we need to step back and look at life and situations realistically — and humor frequently helps us do that.

> "A sense of humor is part of the art of leadership, of getting along with people, of getting things done."
> - Dwight D. Eisenhower

When we try to force fit things and make everything "a matter of life and death," we create a lot of tension for ourselves and those around us. Rather than do a force fit, back off, take a deep breath, and try to view the situation objectively and in the big picture of life (humor can help here). Then think through what makes the most sense for all people involved in solving the problem. There's never an end game as long as we draw a breath and keep thinking (and laughing); there is always time to turn things around, even when time seems to be running out.

BREAKDANCING ON A BALANCE BEAM

> "Life is tough, and if you have the ability to laugh at it you have the ability to enjoy it."
> - Salma Hayek

When you laugh at life and yourself, things somehow start to feel better regardless of the outcome! Laughter can often be the best medicine for changing a tough day into a better one! It brings levity to the moment and can refresh and renew us for the task at hand. Thank you, Bailey, for making me laugh and for providing me with a reality check that wrinkles are signs of aging — but also of wisdom!

BEING ABLE TO LAUGH

Metrics: Do They Always Measure Up?

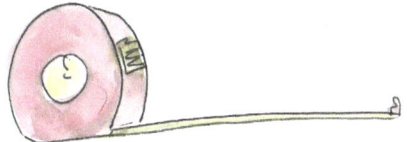

Metrics are everywhere! Today we measure all kinds of things with a speedometer, an odometer, a thermometer, an ergometer, et cetera. In our business and personal worlds these past few years, we are hearing (and learning) constantly about metrics. Business and personal quotes about metrics abound:

> "What gets measured gets done."
> - Attributed to Tom Peters, Peter Drucker, W. Edwards Deming

> "What you need to do is get that tape measure out, and start measuring that gut. Then you start working out and you start eating properly till that gut gets down close to what it was when you were in your 20's. Then you'll find out what your weight should be."
> - Jack LaLanne

Since I continually measure my business numbers, I recently decided to apply that same discipline to the personal side of my life. I invested in a pedometer to see if Jack LaLanne was right.

BREAKDANCING ON A BALANCE BEAM

The instructions with the pedometer suggested it requires about 6,000 steps a day to maintain a constant weight, and about 10,000 to lose weight. After several days of measuring my steps, I noticed I was having a modicum of success with this little device and was quite proud of my numbers, both on the pedometer and on the scale. Then one morning, while rushing to the airport to catch a plane, I noticed that the count-per-step seemed a little "off." I had walked for one hour and it said I had only walked 500 steps, versus the day before when it registered 3,500 steps for the same activity.

After 11 hours of travel in bad weather, I finally arrived at my destination and went to the baggage claim to retrieve my luggage. As I (and 100 other frazzled passengers) stood there waiting, a piercing alarm began to sound on the loud speakers. Passengers covered their ears and asked airport personnel to stop the noise. They tried everything but could not find the source of the racket. An airport employee walked past me and said: "I think it's you that's causing this!" And I said, "Me? I'm just standing here waiting for my bag like everyone else." A man next to me said he had experienced a similar situation in the past when the battery of a passenger's hearing aid ran down, setting off a low-battery warning signal. That signal then entered a feedback loop to the airport's loud speaker system, setting off a similar type of noise.

After I got my luggage and began walking down a desolate hallway towards my car, I realized that the deafening noise was still around me. It was then that I realized: "The Pedometer!" I quickly removed it from my belt and the noise got even louder! I thought for sure airport security would surround me — but there was no one in sight. My morning hunch about the pedometer malfunctioning had proven true — and now this 4-inch pedometer had somehow set off the alarm system throughout the airport terminal!

I hurried to turn it off, but nothing happened. The battery was affixed by a screw and was inaccessible without a screwdriver. I quickly got into my car to get away from the airport, but the noise continued. I then made one of the best metric decisions of my life: I stopped the car, put the pedometer under the front tire, and drove over it!!!

Finally, there was "Peace on Earth"! Needless to say, it was welcome music to my ears. I laughed all the way home while

BEING ABLE TO LAUGH

thinking back to the consternation and annoyed looks on the faces of those passengers in baggage claim. The next morning, I stepped on another measurement device — the scale — and was pleased about what it showed without the noise!

> "If a man does not keep pace with his companions, perhaps it is because he hears a different drummer. Let him step to the music which he hears, however measured or far away."
>
> - Henry David Thoreau

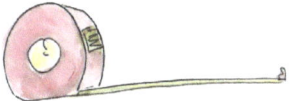

Being Able To Laugh

Laughter is often the best medicine - and the health benefits of a good laugh cannot be overstated. So why is it that we don't make time each day to Find That Laughter?

BEING ABLE TO LAUGH

BEING OPEN TO POSSIBILITIES

Disney calls them "Imagineers"™ — people whose job it is to come up with ideas that fuel the world of creativity that Walt Disney envisioned. It sounds like a dream job, doesn't it? Getting paid to spend your day imagining the possibilities of amazing experiences!

Most of us learn to content ourselves with more mundane jobs. Even when we love what we do, it is important to take actions that keep the excitement alive. The following musings ponder how each of us can become an "Imagineer"™ in whatever we dream of doing. It is about *Being Open To Possibilities.*

As High As A Kite

> "Imagination is the highest kite that one can fly."
> - Lauren Bacall,
>   By Myself and Then Some

Dreams are often the source material for our imaginations. Think how high each of us could fly if we just believed in, and acted upon, the visions and insights from our dreams!! When dreams come true, it is because we feel deeply about them and believe they will. Despite the voices of dissent around us, believers forge on and get up when they fall down, believing that their dreams will ultimately come true.

> "Imagination is more important than knowledge. Knowledge is limited. Imagination encircles the world."
> - Albert Einstein

Good teachers touch the minds and souls of their students. While many choose the profession of teaching, each of us is a teacher to those we meet — be it the gift of a child placed into our care, the person who works with us each day, or the individual we meet on the train who needs our help and direction when they've lost their way.

BEING OPEN TO POSSIBILITIES

By our actions and interactions, we teach each other to grow or shrink, to breathe or gasp for air, to come alive or die, to believe or doubt — and yet all of these yins and yangs help each of us become who we are.

Teachers care for the beautiful minds of children and can open them to the possibilities of life or limit them by building walls and boundaries. The key is finding that right balance between rules and possibilities — bridging the two to foster creativity and imagination that can grow and flourish. Imagination is not for a magical world inhabited by the few. We all use our imaginations in our daily activities whether planning a vacation or a meeting, developing a presentation or solving a problem at work or home.

I have a granddaughter who, when asked what she wanted for a recent birthday said: "A mechanical pencil and some masking tape." At first I looked at her and said: "Are you for "real?" And she said with utmost confidence: "That's really all I want." Needless to say I went to town and bought her an array of colored masking tapes that made me smile at the checkout counter when I received a bill for $13.99.

When she opened her gift, she smiled and immediately ran to her bedroom where she created a beautiful headband, purse and skirt — and a picture frame for me so I could take her picture in her new creation! This little girl tapped her imaginative and creative world and showed me how something as simple as masking tape could be transformed before my eyes into a pretty outfit on a beautiful little girl who smiled at her creativity and sense of purpose and beauty.

> "I saw the angel in the marble and carved until I set him free."
> - Michelangelo on his David

As we go to work or school each day, just remember — the power of imagination is within us to be who we were meant to be. Recall that necessity is the mother of invention (another term for imagination). This means that when we really need to do something, we will figure out a way to do it. Even daily, mundane problem-solving involves use of the imagination.

BREAKDANCING ON A BALANCE BEAM
> So let's create our own worlds with discipline, a sense of purpose, belief in our deeply felt imaginings and, with fun, let them become reality!

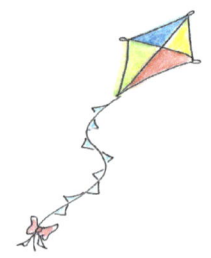

BEING OPEN TO POSSIBILITIES

Slightly Out Of Sync

We all have friends, acquaintances or family members who are just "slightly out-of-sync." At concerts, they clap their hands in between everyone else. In day-to-day life, they make comments that would shock or offend in a typical relationship. While most of the time many of us "swim with the school" and observe social niceties and conventions, there are those individuals who seem to wander off by themselves and those who march to the beat of a different drummer.

In day-to-day activities, we may try to avoid these people because we perceive them as "different." However, while these unique souls can take more effort on our part to get to know and understand, they frequently can bring new and different insights to the most common of occurrences or relationships. They may give us new understandings if we are willing (and able) to take the time to get to know them.

In our fast-paced world, we tend to expect people to respond in a certain way to given situations or interactions. When someone does not, we are likely to disregard them (and/or their input) and move on. This is a little bit of behavior left over from our teenage years where conformity was prized and difference was shunned. It is also a bit of the "herd instinct" which helps to protect us all as a group, but does not encourage individual thought and action.

However, when we get in situations where we cannot ignore the "outlier" (maybe because they're a boss or a close relative) and are required to communicate with them, it is frequently revealing what insights and understandings their different approach can give us. We may not want to march to that drummer ourselves,

BREAKDANCING ON A BALANCE BEAM

but it does give us pause to reflect and realize that our views may not be the only ones, or the only correct ones, or even the best / most valid ones on a given topic.

When we have a lull in activity and life gets more relaxed, seek out that "out-of-sync" friend, relative or colleague and establish communication. You may be amazed at how much you learn from their different perspective. It may not always bring warm, positive feelings but it will bring new insights on, and challenges to, the established order or way of doing things. Such insight is always good for our own development as well as for the communication skills of that different drummer.

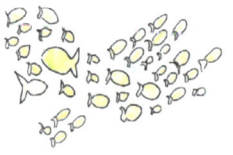

BEING OPEN TO POSSIBILITIES

Maximize YOUR Impact

Y   Yes we can choose to walk our own path

O   Open the door and let others in

U   Use our (and their) time well

R   Remain open to the possibilities

Recently I spent a working vacation (an oxymoron of sorts) at an idyllic bed and breakfast located on the shores of Pleasant Bay in Cape Cod, Massachusetts. I awoke each morning to a beautiful sun rising out of the sea behind a sailboat moored near the water's edge — a view often pictured by artists and storytellers (Homer's "rosy-fingered dawn") — and yet it seemed to be all mine during those precious few minutes. This vacation gave me an opportunity to step back from the pressures of everyday life and reflect on how quickly time passes and how important it is to **Maximize YOUR Impact** during the short time we have on earth.

To do that effectively, it is important to understand, first and foremost, who we really are — our strengths, character, personality and intellect, our behavioral style, and our positives and negatives (we all have them) in dealing with and relating to others. With these insights, we are then able to decide how we will live our lives. This often takes courage and is not easy, but it will at least

BREAKDANCING ON A BALANCE BEAM

be *our* life and *our* impact.

Lest this sound too self-centered, we soon come to understand that we cannot go it alone — although oftentimes many of us might prefer that route. When we let others in, it will give us different ways of looking at and/or approaching things than we might have done otherwise. And often others can pick us up when we fall down or keep us from soaring too near the sun — like the mythical Icarus — and plunging to our ruin. Others enable us to realize Horace's "*golden mean*" — the desirable middle between two extremes — in our living.

And as we all come to know, time is the essence of life. When we are young, it never seems to go fast enough — *"I can't wait till I'm a teenager; I can't wait till I can drive; I can't wait to get out of the house and be on my own..."* And yet when we look back, we often wish we could get a "do over" to either enjoy it again or change a past choice. In reality, the only time is NOW and as Ben Franklin said:

> "If you love life, then do not squander time,
> for that is the stuff life is made from."

Lastly, even when we seem at our wit's end — when the sailboat has broken from its mooring and is adrift, and the sunrise is blocked from view by storm clouds and high seas — that is the most important time to remain open to the possibilities that are always there if we allow them in and don't block them out with negative thinking. So **Maximize YOUR Impact** in life by heeding the words of the intrepid explorer, Christopher Columbus:

> "You can never cross the ocean unless you
> have the courage to lose sight of the shore."

BEING OPEN TO POSSIBILITIES

A Clear Forecast

When I arrived at the airport last week, the agent greeted me with a smile and said, "You picked the right day to be flying. Tomorrow's forecast is stormy, and it will be chaotic. As for today, it's a clear forecast."

When we work and toil each day, we are always looking for that clear forecast. But if we don't occasionally experience stormy conditions in day-to-day work (and life), how can we appreciate the smooth sailing when the chaos subsides?

As we leave one year and look ahead to the next, it will serve us well to review the past year's experiences so we can create a clear forecast for moving forward. To paraphrase Benjamin Zander in his book, *The Art of Possibility*, "It's the silence between the notes that helps us appreciate the music."

So whenever the next year...or event...or phase in your life approaches, try to give yourself some time to enjoy a clear forecast in the midst of the chaos. Reflect on how we need both the chaos and the smooth sailing to succeed in creating (and enjoying) the "music" that's right for us.

The Bridge Is Out!

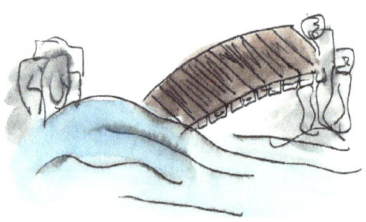

In business, we often have to learn how to bridge the gap to make things work — but what happens when the sign says the "Bridge is Out?" This actually happened to me recently on a weekend visit to a barrier island in North Carolina. A cable on the bridge broke, and we learned from travelers who had tried to leave the island that there was no other way off the island.

At times like these we see the best and worst come out in people! Some people see the negatives in a situation; other people rise to the occasion and look for opportunities and solutions. My group initially cursed our bad luck, but then we began to assess and plan our options — ranging from a long stay on the island (food rationing, waiting it out while enjoying the water and the views), to exploring various ways of getting off the island other than the bridge (swim, wait for low tide, rent a boat or even a helicopter).

In January 2009, US Airways Flight 1549 developed catastrophic trouble over the Hudson River in New York City. Captain Chesley ("Sully") Sullenberger immediately knew that the plane was going down and that people were counting on him to provide the answer that would save them. Rather than wait and waste critical time, he reached deep within and acted on his knowledge, experience, and training to identify the best solution to bring Flight 1549 down safely. He took action, even though he — in his humanness — most likely had a lot of uncertainty about whether his plan would work. He helped people "walk on water" and create "a bridge" to safety. Sully was stalwart in his time of adversity and exemplified

BEING OPEN TO POSSIBILITIES

the words of Jim Rohn:

> "Discipline is the bridge between goals and accomplishment."

The "bridge" can only be permanently out when there are no options. Some of those options are scary; some can be fun; some can be treacherous and outrageous; but *all* are better than saying, "There's nothing we can do." Imagination and creativity in times of crisis and uncertainty are critical for turning obstacles into opportunities. Some common reactions to the "Bridge is Out" scenario include:

- Complain and point the finger at the other guy: "You can't find good help anymore."

- Say: "Why did this happen to me? What did I do to deserve this?"

- Wait it out until it's fixed and just enjoy the water and the view!

- Build a kayak or a plane or a new bridge.

- Use the discovery and rescue plan that you've practiced for situations like this

- Be like Tom Hanks in the movie *Cast Away*: create an imaginary friend and talk to it — it just might help you get through, even when the rough seas are endless and hope seems like it's fading with each sunset!

There are *always* options — having an open mind to the possibilities that exist is the challenge. If we act instead of questioning ourselves to death, who knows? The outcome might just surprise us — just as Captain Sully did. As Winston Churchill said:

> "Attitude is a little thing that makes a big difference."

So the next time your "bridge is out," picture a solution that can take you where you want to be in ways you've never imagined or tried before!

On A Wing And A Prayer

As I traveled home from a business trip, I had to endure the typical discomforts of modern air travel: I paid a $25 fee to check my bag; I crammed into a tight window seat overlooking the wing with little leg room for comfort; the passenger in front of me reclined his seat all the way, pushing my computer into my rib cage. Then we sat on the runway for what seemed an eternity due to flight delays caused by inclement weather. When we finally took off in the fog and rain, the flight attendants announced that once we were at cruising altitude, they would be serving non-alcoholic beverages for $2 and cocktails for $7. In that moment, I realized how much travel and life in general had changed.

Then to my surprise, I looked out the window and my whole view of the world also changed! We were above the clouds, bathed in sunshine and cruising in azure blue skies. It was then that I saw the beauty of the airplane's wing and offered a silent prayer for:

- The soldiers on that plane who were heading home on furlough. They were laughing and spontaneous, yet disciplined and courteous. I thank and honor each one of them for their dedication and courage.

- The little ones on that plane and the wondrous life that lay ahead of them.

BEING OPEN TO POSSIBILITIES

- The young and old passengers alike who were, literally, going forward with their lives.

- Global healing and understanding.

- Being alive and living the life that is mine and mine alone.

As the plane started its descent, life continued its journey. I was still in the same seat as when we took off, but my perspective had changed and I was reminded, once again, to value the moment.

A Light At The End Of The Tunnel

> "It is not the strongest of the species that survives, nor the most intelligent that survives. It is the one that is the most adaptable to change."
> - Charles Darwin

On October 14 and 15, 2010, the world looked on with awe and a sense of unity as it welcomed "los 33" Chilean coal miners back as they were raised one-by-one to the surface in a red, white, and blue rescue capsule called The Phoenix. During their 69-day ordeal of entrapment a half-mile beneath the Atacama Desert, "los 33" were faced with many critical decisions and challenges as they learned how to (successfully) manage their confinement.

As the days crept forward and communications with the outside world were reestablished, it was amazing to hear how *together* these coal miners were. They built a team that was able to understand and address the needs (both spiritual and otherwise) of its individual members by creating a structure of interdependence, self-reliance, and trust. It was equally amazing that in the end, this self-created team made the decision to share equally any proceeds received from the telling of their experience in the media, publications or film.

BEING OPEN TO POSSIBILITIES

To survive, the miners needed to work together to achieve a successful outcome despite their inner, individual beliefs that there was a strong possibility they might not make it out alive! This drama speaks to the creativity and resiliency of the human spirit: How, even in the most difficult of times, there can be a way out and a *light at the end of the tunnel*. It demonstrates how these men could *choose* to live or to die. "Los 33" clearly chose to live — to adapt — and together they were able to make a plan and process that let them succeed. It is a testament to the individual and team spirits. It demonstrates how we really do need each other to survive, but we must act individually as well. Each team member must contribute and hold themselves accountable, or it will not work.

Life's journey is all about interdependence, especially in our increasingly globalized world. So too, in this case, while the world's focus tended to be on the men underground, there was an equally compelling drama of individual initiative and teamwork taking place on the surface. Other members of the "los 33" team were the many people who worked tirelessly and diligently to raise them up from the depths of the mine. They are the unsung heroes in this expedition, many of them Americans with specialized knowledge, expertise and creativity. As in all walks of life, these unsung heroes continue to bring good to this world but do not seek (or need) recognition or to be in the limelight.

A wonderful portrait was painted by this recent saga in all of our minds. Each participant was an artist who put a touch of color on the canvas to create a beautiful painting. The passion for life exhibited by these miners and their rescuers is a work of art that will be remembered around the world for many years to come.

Being Open To Possibilities

Why do we often seem to settle for the routine and ordinary, when there are so many EXTRAORDINARY possibilities out there? What might happen if we Open Our Minds To Those Unlimited Possibilities?

BEING OPEN TO POSSIBILITIES

VALUING CREATIVITY AND INNOVATION

In my line of business, one of the most important skills I have had to develop, refine, and continually hone, is my creativity. Face it, who would listen to a consultant who is boring? It's a challenge to engage an audience, capture their undivided attention, and then hold it for hours, or even a couple of days. Not an activity for the faint-of-heart or dull-of-mind!

Being creative takes work — sometimes lots of work. Oftentimes those creative juices are about as hard to dig up as water in the Mojave Desert! But after spending a lot of time thinking about creativity (and being creative), I have come to some conclusions about it, and I'd like to share them with you.

BREAKDANCING ON A BALANCE BEAM

Creativity: The New C And The Box

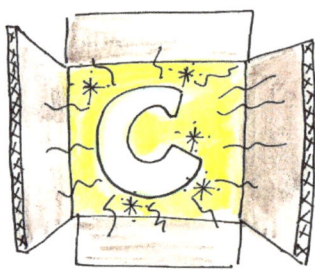

Years ago, I asked participants in a leadership retreat to read a book by Frank A. Prince, called *C and the Box: A Paradigm Parable*. "C", the leading character, wants to get outside the comfortable "box" of familiar habits — to break free of old assumptions in order to grow and develop. The book describes how C really wanted to get out of the box but was afraid and blamed the box for holding him back. C kept peeking up over the rim of the box and saw others being successful by changing and growing, but he stayed trapped in his box.

The "box" is a product of C's own fears (fear of change, fear of growth, fear of trying new things) that limits his vision to see creative ways for getting outside the box or to expand it. As the late Twyla Tharp, renowned choreographer, states in her book, *The Creative Habit*:

> "You can't just dance or paint or write or sculpt. Those are just verbs. You need a tangible idea to get you going. The idea, however miniscule, is what turns the verb into a noun — paint into a painting, sculpt into a sculpture, write into writing, dance into a dance."

VALUING CREATIVITY AND INNOVATION

Creativity, the "New C and the Box," lies within each of us. I recently taught a management workshop in which a participant said to me, "I thought creativity was a skill. But, you are saying it's a behavior that lies within each and every one of us and that with the right environment and preparation we can tap into not only our own creativity but the creativity of those around us." My answer was "YES"— and it is up to each of us to first learn what is present in our own box and identify what we may need from that box to release our own creative potential.

Each of us needs to understand how to tap into our own creativity — first, by realizing that each of us is unique and creativity for one is not necessarily the same for another. It is often individual diversity which, when purposefully harnessed, can create cutting-edge ideas and action.

Creativity is often thought to be a solo enterprise — the novelist, the painter, the musical composer. However, the most common forms of creativity take place every day among groups of people, whether in a family, a business enterprise, a sports team, or any other human collaboration. As the world's knowledge continues to expand in quantum leaps and we become more interdependent, most great creative jumps will require contributions from many people. It is critical that we realize what might be nurturing (or killing) to us might be the opposite for someone else.

Twyla Tharp also said,

> "...before you can think out of the box, you have to start with a box...the box doesn't compose or write a poem or create a dance...but there is one final benefit to the box: it gives you a chance to look back... and reflect on your performance...if you want to know how any creative project will turn out, your box's contents are as good a predictor of success or failure as anything I know. The key is to always be filling that box with ideas that someday may help you create a new painting, writing, sculpture, dance [or business]."

The box is a metaphor for ourselves — our ideas, experiences, relationships, and insights. When we peek into the box and then jump outside of that box, we discover for ourselves the creativity

BREAKDANCING ON A BALANCE BEAM

that lies within. We then need to bring it out and express it. At times we may realize that the creativity we've put forth may not be the creative answer that was needed at that time. However, the action that was taken is not lost. It will help to fill your box with another idea that may ultimately move you one step closer to creative success.

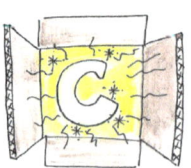

VALUING CREATIVITY AND INNOVATION

YART Sale

Have you ever wanted a fun, creative, and spontaneous life? Have a YART sale!!! Now what in the world is a YART sale? Well, I said the same thing recently when I was taking an early morning run on the cobblestoned streets of Brown University in Providence, Rhode Island. As I jogged through this idyllic area with the sun rising in the distance, I turned a corner and came upon a storefront sign that immediately caught my eye: "YART Sale — This Friday." My initial (and, soon-to-be obviously narrow) thought was, "What morons!!! These people don't know how to spell!" Then, after seeing where the sign was placed — in the window of an ART store...and realizing I was in a very intellectual and clearly artistic community, the light dawned on Marblehead (I know, it's 65 miles northeast of Providence — but the expression seemed to fit!) that *I* was the less-than-intelligent person.

I laughed at myself and was duly impressed at the subtle creativity staring me in the face. It also reminded me how easily we can get caught up in our own narrow thinking and lose sight of the big picture (literally and figuratively, in this case!). This incident prompted me to revisit a few quotes on the subject:

BREAKDANCING ON A BALANCE BEAM

> "Where there is an open mind, there will always be a frontier."
> - Charles F. Kettering

> "Creativity is allowing yourself to make mistakes. Art is knowing which ones to keep."
> - Scott Adams, *The Dilbert Principle*

> "The essence of genius is to make use of the simplest ideas."
> - Charles Peguay, French writer

"YART Sale — This Friday" is a definite keeper. During the past 20 years as a teacher and consultant, I have thoroughly enjoyed my role in guiding students to objectively understand themselves and the diversity of others from a behavioral perspective. I emphasize that creativity and out-of-the-box thinking lies within every one of us. How we express it differs from person to person: Some of us jump right in; others need coaching and encouragement to reach deep within to find what is theirs and theirs alone. Then there are those who leave masterpieces of insight and understanding that we treasure and build upon from generation to generation.

The critical dynamic for teachers is finding and nurturing the creativity within each student, to enable them to share their creative gifts in their own way and, more importantly, in their own time. Some words from a very astute and creative six-year-old: "When I play, it gets me smart for my homework." So go play; have fun; be creative and get smart at that "YART Sale — This Friday"!!! I certainly did!

VALUING CREATIVITY AND INNOVATION

Great Teachers And Great Artists

Do teachers and artists have a common gift? When my son was a freshman in college and adjusting to his first semester away from home — learning to set his own limits and schedules for partying, studying, communal living, and growing up — I remember how one of his teachers captured his mind and raised the bar on his creativity and desire for learning. When he called home, the conversation would always end with his enthusiasm for this one class and how much he loved this professor. About three-quarters of the way through that semester, this special teacher had a heart attack in class and died. I remember hearing and seeing the sense of loss and confusion that my son and his classmates experienced. They questioned the tragedy: *"How could this have happened to someone so good and so young? Why did this happen? What do we do now?"*

At the memorial service, a fellow professor gave the eulogy, a part of which was:

> "...School is not easy or, for the most part, very much fun. But then, if you are lucky you may encounter a great 'teacher.' Three really great teachers in a lifetime are the very best of luck. I have come to believe

that a great teacher is a great artist and that there are as few of them as there are great artists. Teaching might even be the greatest of the arts since the medium is the human mind and spirit. My three 'great' teachers had this in common: They all loved what they were doing. They did not tell — rather they catalyzed a burning desire to know. Under their influence the horizons sprung wide and fear went away and the unknown became knowable. But most of all, the truth — that dangerous stuff — became beautiful and precious. That is what this professor who has been taken from us was able to give to the many young minds who had the good fortune to take his classes."

Great teachers are as rare in the workplace as in the classroom. It takes courage, resilience, civility, and strength of character to take the time to understand yourself and your colleagues, to challenge your and their thinking, and to energize your and their spirit in a constructive and passionate way. In a sense, we are each teachers (as well as students) of our own lives. We are all painting our own unique masterpiece every day, and if we continuously search for the subjects and colors that energize us, we will become that rare artist (or teacher) who can make a difference — as this professor did — in someone else's life. That was his — and could be our — legacy.

Now is the time to be creating the masterpieces we want our lives to be. Make them *our* own! Rose Tremain, the English writer said, "Life is not a dress rehearsal."

We must go out there and create our own unique visions, make them our own and have them make a difference to the lives of those with whom we come in contact.

VALUING CREATIVITY AND INNOVATION

"The teacher who is indeed wise
Does not bid you to enter the house of
his wisdom, but rather leads you to the
threshold of your mind."
- Kahlil Gibran

"All art requires courage."
- Anne Tucker

What Is A Lemon?

> "Nothing exists in isolation.
> We have to stop pretending we are individuals who can go it alone."
> - Margaret Wheatley,
>   *Leadership and the New Science*

One of the topic assignments in my college English Composition course was, "What is a Lemon?" My first thought was, "Is this professor for real? I have so much more creativity and insight to offer the world than being constrained to write about a 'mere' lemon!" I anguished over writing that composition for days before I finally sat down and put pen to paper. I talked to friends and relatives and asked for their perspectives on a lemon. I went to the library to research lemons. I then bought a lemon to touch, squeeze, peel, taste, and smell. As simple as the topic may seem, I had to research using the dictionary and books (pre-Internet days!!), and talk to countless people to gain their insights and perspectives on what they saw a lemon to be. Much to my chagrin, my ideas just didn't flow.

After exhausting my research, I decided to "Just Do It"™ and write that ridiculous composition. I recall how easily my mind's creative juices (no pun intended!) were unleashed and how the ideas began to flow. I was then able to draw with words — in a fun and imaginative way — a vivid picture of a lemon and its impact on such things as iced tea and the laws of our country.

VALUING CREATIVITY AND INNOVATION

A colorful, sour and, at times, bitter lemon became interconnected with beautiful landscapes, icing on a cake, marvelous martinis, and fragrant scents!

Looking back, I now know that the "A" grade I received on that paper was not mine alone. It belonged to the many people (both in books and in person) who gave me their input and enabled me to discover — through discipline, creativity, knowledge, and communication — the inner essence of that lemon. It also belonged to my professor who taught me that being confined to a seemingly limited assignment with such small boundaries can force one to focus and think outside the box…and that necessity is the mother of invention!

Something as simple as a lemon and how we interact with it can make a huge difference in whether we are an "A" or a "D" player in this business called Life. We really can't go it alone. Think how much more important our interactions with each other are than with a lemon! Our interconnectedness and how we manage and tap into it will make a difference in making life hard or simple. Which do you prefer? When life hands you lemons, be positive and creative!

BREAKDANCING ON A BALANCE BEAM

Valuing Creativity And Innovation

Creativity lies within each one of us. How can we value Creativity And Innovation if we're afraid to try it ourselves?

VALUING CREATIVITY AND INNOVATION

BELIEVING IN YOURSELF

My final reflections in this book are very near and dear to my heart: *Believing In Yourself*. I have spent the past 20 years trying to balance my desire to be an entrepreneur — starting, developing, and expanding my own business — with my (equally compelling) desire to be the very best mother, wife, sister, and friend that I can be. Sometimes attaining and sustaining these goals feels like trying to breakdance on a balance beam.

Every inch of success is tempered by the need to change direction, modify goals and behaviors and adapt to the unplanned. But through it all, the single most important thing I have learned is to accept and celebrate the unique person that I am. I hope these thoughts will resonate with you, and will spark in you that same feeling of *Believing In Yourself.*

BREAKDANCING ON A BALANCE BEAM

An Invisible, But Powerful, Force

Recently I was watching the final round of the British Open being played at Royal St. George's Golf Club. The club sits on the southeast coast of England near the cliffs of Dover. That day the wind was howling off the English Channel at about 30mph. One of the commentators said that the wind was "*an invisible, but powerful, force*" that would have a tremendous impact on the outcome of the golf tournament that day.

The phrase about *an invisible, but powerful, force* stuck in my mind as I began thinking about the many such forces that we encounter in our lives every day. At least with the wind, while we may not see it, we can feel it through the broad sense of "touch." How do we sense, read or interpret the "invisible, but powerful, forces" that pummel us each day of our lives?

Each of us is constantly thinking...sometimes consciously and, frequently, subconsciously. These thoughts are invisible to others until we express them or act on them, but they certainly have powerful influence on our lives and often on the lives of others. Even then, our ability to capture and accurately articulate our thoughts is not always on point; when we express our thoughts through our actions, it may be an even murkier message for our fellow human beings to understand and interpret.

So too, the spoken word is invisible but can exert great power as the expression of our thoughts about ideas, events or people. In the complex make-up of human beings, there are many other powerful but invisible forces such as emotions, motivations, biases and viewpoints which we may not even be conscious of because they have been ingrained in us since childhood and have become part of our "unexamined life."

Just as the golfers had to "read" the invisible, but powerful, wind and adjust their play to it in order to succeed in the tournament, so too must we read the many invisible, but powerful, forces that come at us daily to succeed in our human relationships. This is the challenge of human communication and understanding! It is the thrill we get from great literature or even good books which, in communicating a story, give us some insight and understanding of human thoughts and emotions.

And we should not always externalize this process. At times, we should turn it inward to examine and understand our own thoughts, emotions, motivations, biases and viewpoints. This will help us to better understand who we are and what we truly want and need for happiness and fulfillment. It will also enable us to communicate better and thus lead richer, fuller lives. May we all become better readers of the human winds!

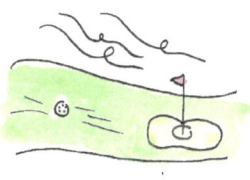

Hire Power

When searching for a new job, how often do we visualize the perfect dream job and then "sit on it" (Ready, Aim, Wait!)? At the other end of the spectrum are those who react immediately, without taking the time to prepare and plan for what they really want and need (Ready, Fire, Aim!).

The best approach lies somewhere in between: Finding a balance between planning and action will help each of us reach our "Hire Power" — our unique wants and needs that, when met, will enable us to perform at our full potential with enjoyment and enthusiasm.

The most important element for achieving our individual Hire Power is understanding ourselves. What we want and need ultimately determines what we can and will achieve in our jobs, our career and our life. Taking stock of who we are may, to some, seem selfish. However, if we don't understand who we are, how will we ever know what we want and need to be fulfilled and contribute to this world? It really is all about *us*!

Instead of worrying about what questions you will be asked in an interview, take charge of the process by thinking about what you want and need from a job, a team and a company. Witness how many people go to work and are just "there" — with no exuberance, zest or engagement for their role. We can blame this on their employer or their team or their job, but the reality is we are responsible for our own lives. We alone can create the changes in ourselves to make our work meaningful and satisfying. However, people do not change until they are motivated to do so — and that motivation comes from within each one of us.

In her book *The Truth About Managing Your Career...and Nothing but the Truth*, Dr. Karen Otazo states:

> "It is a workplace myth that most people are ambitious to get ahead — one reinforced by a culture of promotion meaning success. The truth is that different people are motivated by and committed to different things. The best bit of career planning you will ever do is to spend some time getting to know yourself."

Now is an excellent time to take stock of our most important inventory — ourselves — to see how the year is progressing in honoring and developing our uniqueness. It is as good a time as any to think about what our behavioral needs are and whether they are being met.

So many people today depend on the company to give them the job and then to help them be successful. However, it is up to each of us to identify our own Hire Power and continually work to achieve it, both on and off the job.

In an introspective review, we should ask ourselves:

- What do I need at work?
- What do I want from work?
- What am I most excited about at work?
- Can doing my job well and with enthusiasm help me fulfill my personal needs and wants?
- Or, should I be looking elsewhere to find satisfaction and fulfillment?
- Isn't it up to each of us to find the answers? If we rely on others to always provide the answers for us, we will never find out who we are or what we are capable of.

BREAKDANCING ON A BALANCE BEAM

There's an old adage: "Do what you love and you will never have to work a day in your life." That's the ultimate Hire Power — we control it. Figure out what we truly want, need, and love (not what the world *tells* us to want, need, and love), and then find the work that best enables you to be our fulfilled self.

Life is short. We need to be proactive and take charge of our lives and our careers. Henry David Thoreau said, "What lies behind us and what lies ahead of us are tiny matters compared to what lies within us."

It really *is* all about *us*! We are, and must always be, our own Hire Power!!

A View From The Top

"The heights by great men reached and kept
Were not attained by sudden flight,
But they, while their companions slept,
Were toiling upward in the night."
- Henry Wadsworth Longfellow

For many of us, success is elusive.

Exactly what *is* success? It is defined as the achievement of something desired, planned or attempted. Thus, it may be short or long term; it may be one act or a series of acts; or one long continuing action or activity. Success can be setting a goal and then achieving it or it may be the activity put forth whether we achieve it or not.

The achievement itself may not be the most important thing for us individually. Rather, the process we go through to achieve the goal may mean the most to us. For example, we may define success as passing an exam; or we may define it as living a good, healthy, purposeful life. The range of definitions for success is nearly infinite and is very personal to each of us and our view of the world.

When we achieve success in our lives, whether in a single action or by ongoing activity, it's the preparation, tenacity and belief that we will achieve it that makes all the difference. During those dark moments when we fear we'll never get there is when we absolutely forge ahead. If we do not, we will not!

BREAKDANCING ON A BALANCE BEAM

The following quotes provide insight on what success meant to these individuals at certain points in their lives and what it can mean for us now and in the future.

"The secret of success in life is for a man to be ready for his opportunity when it comes."
- Benjamin Disraeli

"Success seems to be connected with action. Successful people keep moving. They make mistakes, but they don't quit."
- Conrad Hilton

"To succeed... you need to find something to hold on to, something to motivate you, something to inspire you."
- Tony Dorsett

"It is hard to fail, but it is worse never to have tried to succeed."
- Theodore Roosevelt

"The goal ever recedes from us. Salvation lies in the effort, not in the attainment. Full effort is full salvation."
- M.K. Gandhi

"When you get right down to the root of the meaning of the word succeed, you find that it simply means to follow through."
- F. W. Nichol

"Life is either a daring adventure or nothing. I cannot do everything, but I can do something. I must not fail to do the something that I can do."
- Helen Keller

An Inspiration

For a good part of 2009, Susan Boyle was the rage around the world. She won people's hearts with her beautiful rendition of the song "I Dreamed a Dream" from the play *Les Miserables*, performed on the *Britain's Got Talent* television show. Susan Boyle auditioned with the hope of fulfilling her lifelong dream of winning a recording contract.

When Susan walked on the stage, she was awkward in appearance and approach — definitely lacking that sophisticated star attractiveness and beauty that we expect from performers! However, she had an inner self-confidence and belief that served her well. When Susan told the judges and audience of more than 2000 people that she wanted to be like the famous singer Elaine Paige, the First Lady of British Musical Theatre, they all smirked and rolled their eyes as if to say "Get real!"

But when Susan raised the microphone and started to sing, her beautiful, powerful and loving voice filled the hall and instantly touched the hearts and souls of all who were there. During the course of her performance, it was fascinating to see the judges' and the audience's facial expressions change from disdain and arrogance to one of respect, acclaim and applause. At the end of the song, Susan started to walk off the stage while throwing kisses at the audience! The judges called her back so that they could give their unanimous vote of approval on her performance.

BREAKDANCING ON A BALANCE BEAM

Susan's exquisite voice and humble style moved the audience to give her a standing ovation. One judge called her performance the biggest surprise he has had on the show. He said, "In the beginning everyone was laughing at you; but no one is laughing now. Your performance was stunning and incredible!" Another judge said, "Everyone was cynical and against you in the beginning, but your performance was the biggest wake-up call ever. It was a complete privilege listening to that!" It reminded me of the story of the ugly duckling who turned into a beautiful swan!

In the final analysis, this performance clearly shows how humans are critical beings, prone to quickly judge based on our preconceptions. In reality, many of us might walk past Susan Boyle on the street and not even give her the time of day. And yet, beneath her surface appearance is an unbelievably beautiful voice that had been waiting for 47 years to be heard by the world. Susan is a quality example of a human being who, while having seen the hard side of life, remains positive and undaunted. She is able to fill her singing with her experience and insights. Her persistence and determination to never let go of her dream, has brought her a dream come true while giving the world a lesson in hope — that we must be open to finding beauty in the most simple and unexpected places.

Life is about achieving our dreams by using the innate talents we all have. Susan Boyle gave everyone who saw her perform an inspirational message of hope: Good things can happen when we believe in, and are true to, ourselves.

The Entrepreneur In All Of Us

> "In his 1776 thought-provoking book, *The Wealth of Nations*, Adam Smith explained clearly that it was not the benevolence of the baker but his self-interest that motivated him to provide bread. From Smith's standpoint, entrepreneurs were the economic agents who transformed demand into supply for profits."
> - Zeromillion.com, Dr. Alvin Chan, Research Fellow in Asia

Similarly, the self-interest within each of us drives us to achieve results...*if* we listen and act. We can become that "entrepreneur extraordinaire" of our own lives by paying attention to the unique motivations that speak to each of us.

I started my own business despite having had no background or experience in entrepreneurship. And, quite honestly, there are many days when I still feel like I don't have a clue!!! Over the years I have learned a lot, but there is no question that every day is a new one, with new surprises. I try to take it one day at a time but continually come across situations that need an entrepreneurial, self-motivated spirit to get me through. Reviewing the following list helps to keep me grounded and focused when times get tough:

BREAKDANCING ON A BALANCE BEAM

E Everyone (like it or not) is an entrepreneur of their own life and career. The key is to always be searching for the self-interest that motivates *you*.

N No one can control your life or career — that's *your* job.

T Time waits for no one.

R Raise the bar on what you can do — you might amaze yourself at how capable you really are. "The real contest is always between what you've done and what you're capable of doing. You measure yourself against yourself and nobody else." *Geoffrey Gaberino*

E Engage the help and support of those who believe in you and listen to those who do not with guarded skepticism.

P Pay attention to the little things and the big things will take care of themselves.

R Remember that life is no deposit, no return — you go through it only once.

E Everyone experiences ups and downs — how you manage them makes all the difference.

N Never, ever quit — when you think you've reached the end of your endurance is often the moment before you succeed.

E Endings always have new beginnings. "Though no one can go back and make a brand new start, anyone can start from now and make a brand new ending."
                    -Anonymous

U Upside-down thinking can often give you a fresh, new perspective.

R Roads are different for each of us. There is no right or wrong road — but the key is to act, take one of them and never look back. "If you take too long in deciding what to do with your life, you'll find you've done it."
                    - George Bernard Shaw

In closing, I shall quote the much-maligned Machiavelli: "Entrepreneurs are simply those who understand there is little difference between obstacle and opportunity and they are able to turn both to their advantage."

Playing The Game

Every day we compete — willingly or unwillingly — in the game called *life*. Each day we experience wins and losses. It is disappointing and discouraging when we are unable to achieve a goal, despite our hard work and determination to make it happen. How we respond to that "strike out" will influence the outcome of future goals that we set for ourselves. Oftentimes when we least expect it, fate throws us a curve ball that can, in an instant, change the course of our lives.

The true character of a person shines through in challenging moments. How we *respond* to game-changing events makes all the difference. We can choose to whine and wallow in self-pity, or gather strength from within and from the people who care about us. Sometimes all we can do is hang tough, regroup by drawing on reserves deep within and continue to play. We may not win the game in the traditional sense, but how we play it makes all the difference in our personal game.

Recently I had the honor of visiting a hospital in Atlanta, Georgia that specializes in treating patients who have suffered severe spinal cord injuries. I met and got to know three very special teen-agers. Their injuries could have caused them to be negative and resentful. Instead, they chose to lead their lives in a positive light, encouraging and supporting each other.

On the day of my visit, a young man was being discharged from the hospital after having spent nine months in rehab. He was serenaded by the outstanding nursing team, who dressed in Michael Jackson attire and put this 19-year-old's journey into the lyrics of "Beat It". The nurses sang and performed with creativity,

BELIEVING IN YOURSELF

caring fun, and flare to honor the courage and strength of this young man. The room was filled with love and warmth.

The camaraderie of the patients, the staff and the families was evident. The young patients gathered strength from the optimism, courage, and spirit of one another and everyone else in the room. The 19-year-old aptly stated, "What doesn't kill you makes you stronger." He then presented his "S"uperman towel (symbolizing courage, optimism, and bravery) to the young man whom I was visiting, Anton Clifford . Anton beamed with pride as he accepted his trophy and his new responsibility. (Passing down the trophy towel from patient to patient is a hospital tradition and being the recipient of it is an honor — not unlike a trophy for the MVP in the Superbowl.)

When you see such courage and strength — especially in the very young — it sends a strong message that we can choose to overcome any hardship in life. It also reminded me that while we may *think* we can go it alone, life just doesn't work that way! Playing the game of life well demands courage and perseverance, but also being open to the support and love of those around us.

Those three young patients were a wake-up call for me! I am privileged to have been in their company and thank them for reminding me to pursue my dreams and goals passionately; to always play the game with all the style and grace I can muster; and to enjoy every minute of life — its highs and lows — for as long as it lasts.

Thank YOU, Anton Clifford, for being YOU. You've changed many people's lives with your courageous spirit and upbeat approach to life as you:

- Turn insurmountable obstacles into opportunities
- Step up to the plate everyday and hold yourself accountable
- Hang in there and cope with ongoing chaos
- Have a good laugh to help lighten you (and others) up
- Create and think outside the box
- BREAKDANCE ON YOUR OWN BALANCE BEAM TO YOUR OWN RHYTHM!!

Believing In Yourself

Sometimes attaining and sustaining belief in ourselves feels like trying to
Breakdance On A Balance Beam
- adapting to the unplanned while
Believing In Yourself.
How can we all learn to accept and celebrate our uniqueness?

BELIEVING IN YOURSELF

Epilogue

As I come to the end of this collection, I am already getting excited about what I will write next! Sitting here in the elegant lobby of a hotel where I'm attending a business meeting, my mind is already racing ahead to what the future might hold for me, for my family, for all those with whom I work and for those of you I may have touched with this book. Outside, the sunshine is becoming blurred by the thickening clouds of an approaching storm. But, just now, as the storm nears, that sunshine has turned the world around me into gold. May all of us harvest the gold that comes from knowing and *Believing In Yourself!*

So Go Ahead

and

Breakdance On YOUR Balance Beam

To YOUR Own Beat and YOUR Own Rhythm!

About The Author

A spirited entrepreneur and gifted facilitator, Kathy Frank is Founder and CEO of Augur Inc., an organizational and strategic management consultancy firm with offices in Bedminster, New Jersey. She is an author and developer of numerous proprietary training modules designed to optimize team performance in organizations — from small startups, nonprofits, and educational institutions, to members of the Fortune 500. Kathy is an entrepreneur in the purest sense. She built a million-dollar consulting practice from scratch. She is a dynamic visionary, connector and strategist known for her warmth and resilience in the face of challenges.

As Walt Disney once said,

> *"If you dream it, you can do it."*

Acknowledgements

*My dream of creating this book
would never have been
realized without:*

My Family. I am extremely grateful for their love and support; for putting up with my ups and downs throughout my journey of building Augur Inc. — for their ideas, creativity, and belief in me even when oftentimes I was so unsure!

- **Peter** — my terrific husband — my rock who has a great sense of humor and always makes me laugh — the wind beneath my wings — the behind-the-scenes person who has always been there for me — who gave me a special plaque: *"Be Yourself — No one can ever tell you you're doing it wrong."* _{Charles Schulz}   Peter wordsmithed every article I wrote, and it was our *"team dynamic"* and synergy that helped those articles really come to life.

- **David** — my talented, fun and brilliant son, who with his logical mind and great business acumen told me to stop being a wimp and *Just Do It*™.   He, like his Dad, always believed in me and gave me the strength and wisdom to continue when I faced tough obstacles on my entrepreneurial journey building Augur Inc.

- My daughter-in-law, **Kista**, who gave me a listening ear and helped me by citing Robert Frost's poem, "Two Roads Diverged in a Single Wood" — you can only choose one path.   Just choose it and all the rest will fall into place.

- My three beautiful grandchildren, **Bailey, Courtney Elizabeth** and **Connor**, who with their innocence and zest for life provided so many ideas for these musings; who kept asking me: "*Is your book done yet? Is my name going to be in it?" I want to tell all of my friends about it*"; but most of all they'd say, "*We don't care if you publish a book — we will always love you anyway — but it would be great if you did because you are so much fun and we love your stories.*"

- My sister, **Maryann**, and brother-in-law, **Michael**, who were always interested in how the book was coming along; who listened quietly with love and support to all that was going on in my world.

- My twin brother, **Ed**, someone with great strength of character who has always been there for me — and for his partner, **Sal**, who always provides positive words of encouragement.

- My brother-in-law **Pat Mears**, who always asked how the book was coming and supported this endeavor.

- My courageous niece, **Tricia Mears**, who has her mother's work ethic and creativity and wants to share it with the world in her cinematography; her Mom would be so proud of her endeavors.

- And my terrific nephews, **Michael, Bryan, Edward** and **Patrick,** who will hopefully enjoy reading these musings.

I include as members of my family other people who have encouraged, supported, and helped me realize this dream:

- **Alice Taylor** — my esteemed editor and dear friend. Alice has always been the calm force who listened and gave me strength in low moments. She was the voice of logic and reason when my emotions kicked in — who was able to edit with style and grace these musings and make them real and powerful. She has been a rock in times of change and uncertainty and was never afraid to kick me out of my doldrums — as we enjoyed a glass of wine and friendship.

- **Caitlin Johnson-Nied** — my creative artist. Caitlin is a beautiful, intelligent and phenomenal artist who at a young age realizes that life has so much to offer and she is not afraid to seize it. Her strong work ethic, positive approach to life, can-do attitude and her keen ability to adapt to almost any situation and make it work will bring her rich rewards. She was never frazzled by my many changes and was quickly able to create new ideas that worked!

- **Jeanne Walsh**, who helped me get every article out on schedule despite my belatedness in sending them her way — she also provided input and suggestions for change in each article.

- **The team at Augur**, Elizabeth Faircloth, Joan Mueller, Jeanne Walsh, Molly Lee, Kathy Phelan, Cathy Yonki, Joan Munro, Alice Taylor, Caitlin Johnson-Nied, Jill Stropoli. Julie Hagovsky and Chris Miles, who supported my efforts and were thankful that we had a marketing piece out there every month that was shared with clients and which clients enjoyed.

And then there are:

- **My many mentors** who gave willingly of their time and energy to improve my dance routine along the way: Arnold Daniels, Andrea Novakowski, Brad Swift, Charlie Currie, Dave Hickey, Mike Dunn, Joyce Bushey, Elizabeth Faircloth, Joan Mueller, Molly Lee, Alan Weiss, Leslie Segal, Sally Muscarella, Mark Alexander, Barb Murphy, Mindy Goldberger, Michelle Cameron and Sr. Maureen Fay, Dr. Mary O'Neill, Sharyn Whitman, Celia Clifford, Ruedi Affentranger, Betty Ryan, Angela Zimmerman and Vicki Cerami. They ALL told me in their own words: "If there's a book in you — Write it!! Don't just dance around it!"

- **Augur Inc.'s Advisory Board** who gave of their time and expertise to my business at no charge — my unsung heroes! They provided ongoing support and their guidance helped me countless times to figure out how to balance the chaos and calm that can make or break a business. Their only request of me in return: "Be Open. Listen. Learn. Then Decide." Each of them became a catalyst that helped me grow my business from nothing to where it is today — Mike Keating, Wade Tambor, John Sebastiano, Peter Donnelly and Elizabeth Mallory.

- **The people who, for eight years, have read my monthly e-newsletters** and told me I should write a book — "You have a wonderful message to share that has a human side that touches people's lives."

There is a book in all of us — we're writing it every day — whether we put it to pen or not — it's what we do with this one precious life that makes all the difference to achieving a life well lived. The choice belongs to each of us!!

Order Form

Breakdancing on a Balance Beam by Kathy Frank

 e-mail orders: Orders@baileycourtcon.com

 Fax orders: + 877-497-3369

 Telephone orders:　Call +1-877-497-3369

 Postal orders: P.O. Box 8206, Bedminster, NJ　07921
USA

See our website www.baileycourtcon.com for information on speaking engagements/seminars/mailing lists, consulting.

Name:

Address:

City, State/Province/Postal Code:

Tel:

Email:

Payment:　Check:　　　　　Credit Card:

Visa　　MasterCard　　Amex　　Discover　　PayPal

Card number:

Exp. Date: (mm/yy):　　　　Security Code: